DISEASES AND DISORDERS

ASTHMA
THE STRUGGLE TO BREATHE

By Peter Kogler

Portions of this book originally appeared in *Asthma* by Barbara Sheen.

Published in 2019 by
Lucent Press, an Imprint of Greenhaven Publishing, LLC
353 3rd Avenue
Suite 255
New York, NY 10010

Designer: Deanna Paternostro
Editor: Jennifer Lombardo

Library of Congress Cataloging-in-Publication Data

Names: Kogler, Peter, author.
Title: Asthma : the struggle to breathe / Peter Kogler.
Description: New York : Lucent Press, [2019] | Series: Diseases and disorders
  | Includes bibliographical references and index.
Identifiers: LCCN 2018015759 (print) | LCCN 2018017775 (ebook) | ISBN
  9781534564930 (eBook) | ISBN 9781534564923 (library bound book) | ISBN
  9781534564916 (pbk. book)
Subjects: LCSH: Asthma–Treatment. | Asthma–Diagnosis.
Classification: LCC RC591 (ebook) | LCC RC591 .K64 2019 (print) | DDC
  616.2/38–dc23
LC record available at https://lccn.loc.gov/2018015759

Printed in the United States of America

CPSIA compliance information: Batch #BW19KL: For further information contact Greenhaven Publishing LLC, New York, New York, at 1-844-317-7404.

Please visit our website, www.greenhavenpublishing.com. For a free color catalog of all our high-quality books, call toll free 1-844-317-7404 or fax 1-844-317-7405.

CONTENTS

Illness is an unfortunate part of life, and it is one that is often misunderstood. Thanks to advances in science and technology, people have been aware for many years that diseases such as the flu, pneumonia, and chicken pox are caused by viruses and bacteria. These diseases all cause physical symptoms that people can see and understand, and many people have dealt with these diseases themselves. However, sometimes diseases that were previously unknown in most of the world turn into epidemics and spread across the globe. Without an awareness of the method by which these diseases are spread—through the air, through human waste or fluids, through sexual contact, or by some other method—people cannot take the proper precautions to prevent further contamination. Panic often accompanies epidemics as a result of this lack of knowledge.

Knowledge is power in the case of mental disorders, as well. Mental disorders are just as common as physical disorders, but due to a lack of awareness among the general public, they are often stigmatized. Scientists have studied them for years and have found that they are generally caused by hormonal imbalances in the brain, but they have not yet determined with certainty what causes those imbalances or how to fix them. Because even mild mental illness is stigmatized in Western society, many people prefer not to talk about it.

Chronic pain disorders are also not well understood—even by researchers—and do not yet have foolproof treatments. People who have a mental disorder or a disease or disorder that causes them to feel chronic pain can be the target of uninformed opinions. People who do not have these disorders sometimes struggle to understand how difficult it can be to deal with the symptoms. These disorders are often termed "invisible illnesses" because no one can see the symptoms; this leads many people to doubt that they exist or are serious problems. Additionally, people who have an undiagnosed disorder may understand that they are experiencing the world in a different way than their peers, but they have no one to turn to for answers.

Misinformation about all kinds of ailments is often spread through personal anecdotes, social media, and even news sources. This series aims to present accurate information about both physical and mental conditions so young adults will have a better understanding of them. Each volume discusses the symptoms of a particular disease or disorder, ways it is currently being treated, and the research that is being done to understand it further. Advice for people who may be suffering from the disorder is included, as well as information for their loved ones about how best to support them.

With fully cited quotes, a list of recommended books and websites for further research, and informational charts, this series provides young adults with a factual introduction to common illnesses. By learning more about these ailments, they will be better able to prevent the spread of contagious diseases, show compassion to people who are dealing with invisible illnesses, and take charge of their own health.

INTRODUCTION

A RECURRING DIAGNOSIS

Asthma is a chronic, or long-term, and incurable disease that affects a person's ability to breathe. During an asthma attack, the airways in a person's nose and mouth swell, reducing the flow of air both in and out of the lungs. It is estimated that more than 300 million people worldwide are affected by asthma, and by 2025, that number is expected to increase to 400 million.

There are no exact numbers on those who suffer from asthma. Asthma is often underdiagnosed by doctors, and in developing countries, there is not enough research and often not enough health care services to study and treat its related effects. In the United States alone, an estimated 18.4 million adults and 6.2 million children suffer from asthma every day.

According to the American Academy of Allergy, Asthma and Immunology (AAAAI), "One in 12 people ... had asthma in 2009, compared with 1 in 14 ... in 2001."[1] An estimated 3,615 people in the United States died from its effects in 2015 alone. The Asthma and Allergy Foundation of America reported, "There is no cure for asthma, but it can be managed with proper prevention ... and treatment."[2]

People who suffer from asthma, who are sometimes called asthmatics, exist all across the globe, and all races, ethnicities, ages, and genders are affected. Those who live in developing countries are more likely to have asthma than those who live in developed countries.

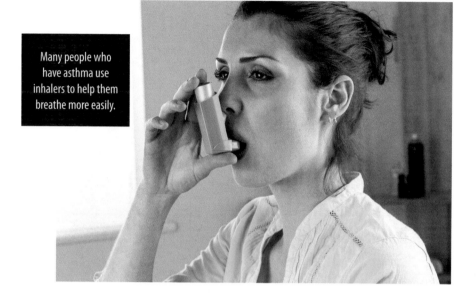

Many people who have asthma use inhalers to help them breathe more easily.

Asthma on the Rise

Diagnosed cases of asthma are increasing as the world continues to grow and develop. According to the Centers for Disease Control and Prevention (CDC), the number of Americans with asthma increased by 28 percent between 2001 and 2011. Similar growth has been seen around the world, including in developing nations. The rise of asthma in developing nations is especially troubling because of the limited access to medical care and asthma treatments. Since uncontrolled asthma can be fatal, this lack of care means a higher percentage of asthma-related deaths.

Furthermore, developing countries tend to have more widespread pollution. This negatively affects the health of all people, but it hits people with asthma especially hard. In 2015, the World Health Organization (WHO) estimated that "there were

383,000 deaths due to asthma"[3] that year. The WHO also reported that this chronic disease is preventable, but not if air pollution continues to increase.

The WHO, whose headquarters in Geneva, Switzerland, is shown here, focuses on the physical, mental, and social well-being of people all around the world.

The Cost of Asthma in America

Because asthma is so prevalent in the United States, it is having an incredible impact on individuals, families, and society. Society as a whole is affected because of the amount of lost work and school days, as well as the burden on the health care system. Asthma costs an estimated $81.9 billion annually in the United States. People with asthma live with the stress of knowing that they can have an attack at any time. Approximately 30,000 Americans have an asthma attack every day, which adds up to about 12 million Americans per year. In the United States, an estimated 10 million doctor and emergency room visits are asthma-related. One out of every four emergency room visits is due to an asthma attack, which equals about 2 million emergency room visits per year.

The disease causes 500,000 hospitalizations per year, with an average three-day hospital stay. Nearly half of these asthma-related hospitalizations are for children. Although asthma is not often life-threatening if someone has access to adequate medical care, it still kills thousands of Americans annually. Asthma also causes an estimated 40,000 absences a day in American schools and workplaces. A student with asthma misses an average of 8 school days a year; altogether, this makes up a total of 14 million missed school days. In fact, asthma is the number one cause of regular school absences. These students can fall behind in their studies, and their teachers lose time having to reteach missed lessons.

The American workplace is also impacted. Workers miss about 14 million workdays annually due to asthma, some of which occur when a parent has no choice but to stay home with a sick child. Some workers with asthma are even forced to quit their jobs because of workplace exposure to substances that trigger their asthma symptoms.

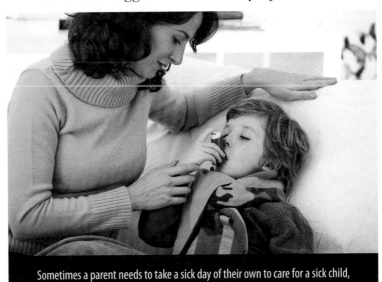

Sometimes a parent needs to take a sick day of their own to care for a sick child, which can have an impact on their job.

Educating the World

Those who suffer from asthma can learn how to manage their disease through treatment and education. This knowledge is essential in keeping their symptoms and level of suffering under control, which in turn helps reduce emergency room and doctor's office visits, as well as school and workplace absenteeism. As friends, family, teachers, and everyone else around the affected person learn about this disease, they

Every year, the Global Initiative for Asthma (GINA) organizes World Asthma Day. This day is intended to spread asthma awareness and education to people around the world.

become able to provide people who have asthma with appropriate support. In some cases, such support and knowledge can help keep asthma symptoms from escalating into a life-threatening asthma attack.

CHAPTER ONE

AN UNCOMFORTABLE ATTACK

The bodies of people who suffer from asthma are overly sensitive to any number of substances or activities. These substances or activities are known as asthma triggers. Triggers that affect people with asthma do not normally cause serious problems in other individuals, but in those with the disease, triggers cause their immune system to overreact, and as a result, their airways swell and narrow. This narrowing of the airways makes it difficult to get air in and out of their lungs.

Asthma is a chronic condition. This means that once someone develops asthma, it will have persistent, lifelong effects that will vary in severity. Currently, doctors and researchers know little about what causes asthma, and unfortunately, there is no known cure. There is only treatment and education. Through research, advances in medication and other treatment methods will hopefully make it easier for people with asthma to live more comfortably.

How People Normally Breathe

To better understand how asthma affects the body, it is important to understand how people breathe. The human body relies on a road-like network of about 100,000 tubes to carry air in and out of the lungs. It all begins when a person inhales air through their nose and mouth. Normally when this happens, air is pushed from the mouth and nose down into the throat. The air enters a long, hollow tube known as the trachea, or windpipe. The trachea branches off into two smaller tubes called the bronchi, which connect to both the right and left lungs. The bronchi then branch off into thousands of smaller tubes, known as bronchioles, within the lungs. These bronchioles end in 300 million microscopic air sacs called alveoli. This is where oxygen and carbon dioxide are transferred in and out of the bloodstream.

As the oxygen is used, carbon dioxide is formed and exhaled out of the lungs and body. If a person inhales a harmful substance such as smoke or smog, the airways have a natural defense to protect the lungs. A thin layer of sticky mucus covers the lining of the airways, which traps harmful particles and germs in much the same way flypaper traps insects. Tiny hairs, or cilia, that also line the airways help move the mucus along and out of the body. The mucus and any trapped particles end up in the throat, where they are then expelled from the body through coughing or sneezing.

Mucus that contains particles the body wants to get rid of can be expelled when someone sneezes.

How an Asthmatic Breathes

The airways of a person with asthma are hyper-responsive to the things they breathe in. This means they are overly sensitive to normally harmless substances and triggers. These substances and triggers can include tree pollen, air pollution, cold air, and physical exercise. An asthmatic body treats these triggers as if they posed a threat to the body, and it signals the immune system to react and attack aggressively. Mucus and cilia in this case do not work as expected. As a result, powerful chemicals that cause inflammation, which is the body's main method of fighting harmful organisms, are sent to the airways.

The problem is that this inflammation response does not go away on its own, as the body is mistakenly attacking something harmless. If there were actually an invader, such as a germ, the inflammation would die down after the intruder was destroyed. However, since there is no actual threat to the body, inflammation in people with asthma sets off a dangerous chain of long-lasting events. First, in an effort to get blood with infection-fighting white blood cells to the airways, inflammation causes the linings of the airways to swell. This makes the muscles surrounding the airways twitch and then tighten. As a result, the airways narrow, which reduces the amount of oxygen and carbon dioxide that gets through.

Inflammation stimulates mucus production that would normally help the body rid itself of germs and allergens. However, in an asthma attack, this mucus is unnecessary. It forms plugs in the narrowed airways that make breathing very difficult. This is what causes the noticeable symptoms of asthma, such as coughing and wheezing. Wheezing, a telltale sign of asthma, is a whistling sound that is made as individuals try to push air through the blocked airways. An asthma attack can also include a burning sensation in the chest when the airways narrow. The level of inflammation can vary, so asthma symptoms may be so minor that the person does not even notice them or so severe that they are life-threatening. The more severe the inflammation is, the more severe the symptoms will be.

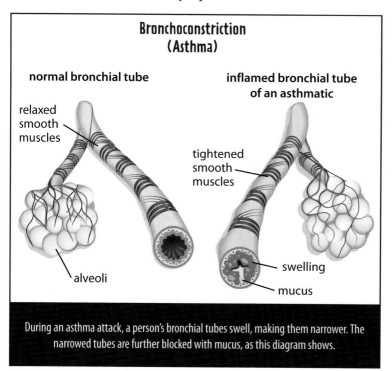

Bronchoconstriction (Asthma)

normal bronchial tube

inflamed bronchial tube of an asthmatic

relaxed smooth muscles

tightened smooth muscles

alveoli

swelling

mucus

During an asthma attack, a person's bronchial tubes swell, making them narrower. The narrowed tubes are further blocked with mucus, as this diagram shows.

Complicating matters, once the airways become inflamed, they become even more sensitive. This sets off a dangerous inflammatory cycle in which the airways can constrict, narrow, and clog much more easily as time goes on. As a result, even when people with asthma feel fine, there is always still some airway inflammation. The feeling of this constant inflammation has been described as "like having a sunburn in your bronchial tubes."[4]

A Dangerous Reaction

Excessive inflammation is what triggers an asthma attack, and the symptoms escalate rapidly. The airways become so narrow and clogged that it takes a lot of effort to get air through them, which makes exhaling difficult. As a result, dangerous carbon dioxide builds up in the body. Too much of this carbon dioxide can be deadly. Making matters worse, this excess carbon dioxide, combined with the constricted airways, makes it difficult for oxygen to enter the body.

Understanding the Immune System

The immune system is the body's defense system against disease. It consists of billions of specialized cells that protect the body from harmful substances, such as bacteria, viruses, fungi, and parasites. When a foreign substance enters the body, the immune system sends white blood cells to the area. There are many types of white blood cells, and each one has a specific job.

Lymphocytes are the first cells that are released. When they come into contact with the invader, they cover it completely. This causes bits of the foreign substance to stick to the lymphocytes. The composition of the foreign substance's protein alerts the immune system to the identity of the invader. If the substance is identified as an antigen—a harmful foreign substance—specialized proteins known as antibodies, each shaped to match up with and lock on to a specific antigen, are released. In the case of asthma, harmless substances such as pollen are mistaken for antigens.

Other white blood cells are also released during an immune response. Neutrophils are the most common, as they attack bacteria. Dead neutrophils are what make up pus, which is the thick, yellowish fluid in a pimple or other infected tissue. Eosinophils and basophils are less common. Eosinophils attack parasites, while basophils are involved in triggering inflammation.

The microscopic basophil, shown here as it would be seen under a microscope, is a type of white blood cell that causes inflammation.

Therefore, during an asthma attack, the person physically struggles to get air both in and out of the body. People having an attack report feeling as if they are slowly suffocating. This frightening and uncomfortable sensation can sometimes cause them to panic as they fight to breathe. However, panicking creates its own problems, such as breathing too rapidly, which is known as hyperventilation. Hyperventilation can further worsen asthma symptoms as well as create dizziness and more anxiety. If an attack is severe, lack of oxygen may turn victims' lips and fingertips blue and cause them to lose consciousness. In extreme cases, this lack of oxygen is what leads to death.

When an asthma attack occurs, the person experiencing it should try to remain as calm as possible, since panicking makes their symptoms worse.

Varying Triggers

Any number of inhaled, ingested, injected, or touched substances, as well as physical activities or emotional factors, can set off the inflammatory process that causes an asthma attack. These are known as asthma triggers. Allergens; pollution; weather extremes; respiratory infections; chemicals found in medicines, cleaning products, or perfumes; exercise; excitement; and stress are all examples of asthma triggers.

Allergens are among the most common asthma triggers. These are generally harmless substances for most people, such as grass, tree pollen, dust mites, mold, and animal dander. People with allergies have immune systems that overreact, much the way people with asthma do. However, an allergic reaction is different from an asthma attack. Allergic reactions can consist of skin rashes, nasal congestion, sneezing, and itchy eyes.

Allergies and asthma are closely connected. In fact, 70 percent of people with asthma have allergies. For these people, the simplest allergens can easily trigger an asthma attack. Individuals whose asthma is triggered by allergens are said to have allergic asthma.

SYMPTOMS

red eyes — swollen throat — runny nose

rash — tearing — sneezing

FACTORS

pollen — animals — insects

fruits — dust — nuts

For people with allergic asthma, any of their allergens may also be an asthma trigger.

Triggers in Everyday Life

Other triggers may not be allergy related. For example, smoke can provoke an asthma attack in many people. Smoke can come from a variety of sources, such as tobacco products, fires, and substances found in polluted air, such as vehicle exhaust fumes and other chemicals.

Everyday products can trigger asthma as well.

Salicylates, chemicals found in aspirin, trigger symptoms in about 10 percent of people with asthma. Sulfites, which are food additives used to preserve beer, wine, dried fruit, and some processed foods, are also known triggers. For unknown reasons, people with severe asthma are especially sensitive to sulfites.

Allergies and Anaphylaxis

An allergy is another type of hypersensitivity disorder. People with allergies are overly sensitive to one or more allergens, which are normally harmless substances that do not cause problems in most other people. This sensitivity causes their immune system to overreact, setting off an inflammatory reaction. An allergic reaction sometimes makes a person feel ill, as the symptoms can include nasal congestion, coughing, sneezing, watery eyes, and headaches.

Anaphylaxis is a life-threatening allergic reaction, and although it is uncommon with those who have allergies, it is very serious. Anaphylaxis occurs suddenly, creating nausea, vomiting, diarrhea, dizziness, trouble breathing, and low blood pressure. If left untreated, anaphylaxis can lead to cardiac arrest and even death. Those who have had this type of reaction even once are more likely to have another similar reaction in the future.

Infections, which activate the immune system, also can trigger asthma symptoms in some people. In fact, the majority of asthma attacks in children are triggered by viral infections. Extreme weather conditions, too, are common triggers. Cold, dry air, for example, causes the airways to contract even in people without asthma. Since the airways of people with asthma are chronically inflamed, anything that causes them to narrow further can be dangerous. Sudden changes in humidity and temperature lead to an increase in reported asthma cases. Something as simple as walking from a warm building into cold winter air can trigger an asthma attack.

Even electricity in the air during thunderstorms and high winds can affect some people with asthma. These weather conditions cause plants to release more pollen and mold spores, which trigger asthma attacks among asthmatics with pollen allergies.

When multiple triggers are present, the likelihood of an asthma attack increases. For instance, having a cold and being outside on a cold, rainy day could trigger an asthma attack, especially if the person just came from a warm, dry building.

Exercise and Emotions as Triggers

Physical exercise triggers some asthma as well. Because exercise causes people to breathe harder and reduces heat and moisture in the airways, the muscles around the airways can tighten. Moisture in the lungs, which is normally replaced when people catch their breath, cannot be replaced in some people with asthma. Physical activities in the winter that involve breathing cold, dry air, such as ice skating, snowboarding, and skiing, are especially problematic.

Normally, people inhale cold air through the nose, where it is warmed and moistened before entering the airways. During winter physical activities, individuals are more likely to breathe through their mouths. When this happens, cold, dry air passes directly into the airways, which can trigger an asthma attack. Therefore, those with asthma should be very careful when participating in cold-air sports.

Strong emotions, such as excitement or sadness, can also trigger asthma. Crying at something sad or laughing at something funny can actually be harmful to someone with asthma. Like physical exercise, laughing and crying reduce moisture and heat in the airways and cause a person to breathe harder, which makes the muscles around the airways tighten.

In the basic human stress response, two hormones in the brain, cortisol and adrenaline, turn on the body's inflammatory system in order to get through a crisis. Early humans needed this response to survive dangerous situations millions of years ago, but for modern-day people, this basic response occurs when they are stressed at home, work, or school. For someone with asthma, this is clearly not beneficial.

Any number of these triggers can cause asthma symptoms in susceptible people. In fact, most people have multiple asthma triggers.

Genetics in Asthma Cases

Asthma triggers do not cause asthma; they cause asthma symptoms in people who already have the disease. Anyone can develop asthma, although some people are at greater risk than others.

Scientists do not know for sure what causes asthma, but they believe genes play a role. People with a family history of asthma are more likely to develop the condition than those who do not. This predisposition is passed down in a person's DNA—the genetic material that determines the makeup of all cells—from parent to child. If a child has one parent with asthma, that child has a 25 to 50 percent chance of also having asthma. If both parents have asthma, that number increases to somewhere between 51 and 80 percent.

The variation in the percentages is due to the fact that more than 100 genes appear to be linked to asthma. Inheriting any of these genes does not guarantee that individuals will develop asthma, but the chance is higher. Scientists believe the more of these genes a child inherits, the higher their risk is of developing asthma—and the higher the severity of their symptoms.

Some of these genes are more common in black people than in other races. This puts many black people, especially black children, at a higher risk of developing asthma. According to the CDC, black children are twice as likely as white children to have asthma and 10 times more likely to die from it. This group is also at a higher risk of developing severe symptoms. Researchers are unsure of exactly why this is, especially since most of the genetic research into asthma has been done on white people, who are less likely to have some of the genes linked to asthma. Medications also work differently for different races. For instance, the asthma medication Advair carries a written warning that using it greatly increases the risk of death for black people. So while this medication may help white patients, it can be dangerous for black patients, which experts say may be one of the reasons

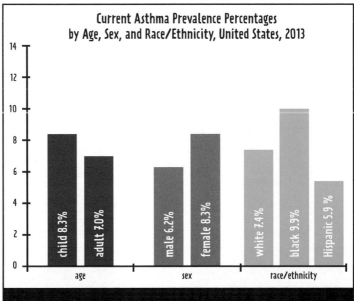

Women, children, and black people have a higher risk of developing asthma than other groups, as this information from the CDC shows.

for the higher asthma death rate in this group. Studies into this issue are ongoing.

Dangers in the American Workplace

Like asthma, allergies run in families and have a genetic link. Some people with asthma, however, do not have allergies or a family history of allergies or asthma. This group includes people in jobs where they are exposed to irritating chemicals on a regular basis. Scientists have identified more than 300 different workplace irritants, including chemical fumes, dust, smoke, gases, animal substances, and metals. Regularly inhaling large amounts of any of these irritants can weaken and irritate the airways and can cause people to develop an allergy to the substance. Scientists think such factors make these individuals more susceptible to developing asthma. However, an estimated 11 million American workers are regularly exposed to at least one of these substances, but not all of them develop asthma. Scientists do not know why this is so.

The irritants people breathe in every day can lead to long-term and short-term negative health effects. Some workers, such as this metal worker, are at a higher risk than others.

According to the U.S. Department of Labor, about 15 percent of all adult asthma cases may be linked to work-related factors. Professions with the highest risk of developing asthma as an adult include firefighters, dry cleaners, textile workers, bakers, hairdressers, painters, construction workers, janitors, and factory workers—all of whom inhale a wide variety of fumes and chemicals in their everyday jobs. Firefighters, for instance, are regularly exposed to smoke, soot, dust, and smoldering wood chips, among other irritants. A three-year-long California study that ended in 2009 found that firefighters reported the third-highest rate of occupational asthma; janitors and dry cleaners were the top two. A 2010 study conducted by the Centre for Research in Environmental Epidemiology in Barcelona, Spain, found that breathing in bleach, ammonia, and stain removers more than once a week, as a dry cleaner would, was linked with a 20 percent rise in asthma.

Adult asthma in field workers has been reported, too, as they often work with chemicals that are sprayed onto machinery and crops. Factory workers and painters often wear special masks to help minimize irritation to their lungs. However, some chemicals are so irritating to the lungs that even slight exposure can cause asthma to develop. Again, although this happens to some people, it does not happen to everyone, and scientists are unsure why some are more susceptible than others. Researchers learn more about asthma every year. It is clear that a number of factors determine who develops the condition and that a wide variety of substances can trigger asthma symptoms.

CHAPTER TWO

IDENTIFYING AND TREATING ASTHMA

Because coughing and wheezing can be symptoms of other illnesses, such as a respiratory infection, doctors cannot use that information alone to diagnose asthma. Patients need to tell their doctors if they are experiencing recurring episodes of coughing, wheezing, chest tightness, and shortness of breath. Doctors will then conduct an examination and run medical tests to diagnose suspected asthma. Once a diagnosis is made, doctors will assess the severity of the case and begin a treatment plan. Treatment involves two types of medicine: a controller medication and a quick-relief medication. The controller medicine prevents an attack, while the quick-relief medication relaxes the airway to make breathing easier.

Seeing a Doctor

The symptoms of asthma can also apply to other diseases and disorders, such as respiratory infections, lung cancer, acid reflux, and some forms of heart disease. This is why a visit to the doctor's office is incredibly important. Medical professionals must eliminate the possibility of all these other conditions before making an asthma diagnosis. Carefully questioning patients, learning their medical history, and giving a physical examination help health care professionals do this accurately.

First, patients are asked to describe their symptoms and how often those symptoms appear. In an infection, the onset of symptoms will be sudden. Symptoms can also be seasonal, constant, or seen after exposure to certain substances or triggers. Questions about a patient's allergies, work history—where they may be exposed to irritants daily—and family health history will also help a doctor make a diagnosis. A physical examination will follow, where the doctor will look at lungs, airways, and nasal discharge and swelling (which are both signs of allergies or infections). A chest X-ray may also be administered. This gives a clearer picture of the lungs and can help rule out lung cancer.

The Spirometry Test

A doctor may then perform a spirometry test on the patient, which measures how well the lungs are functioning. During the test, a patient will blow into a tube-like device that is attached to a computer. The computer measures the person's airflow, which is the speed and volume of the air the patient exhales. The measurement is compared to normal airflow for a person of the same age, gender, height, and race as established by the American Thoracic Society.

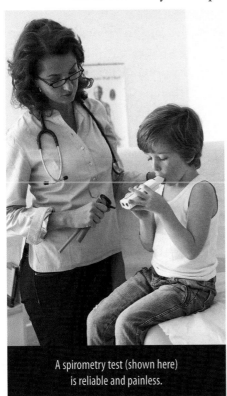

A spirometry test (shown here) is reliable and painless.

The patient will do this at least three times, which ensures a consistent measurement. If the airflow is less than normal, the patient is treated with a bronchodilator—a quick-acting asthma relief medication that opens up the airways—and then performs the spirometry test again. If the patient's airflow increases significantly the second time, it suggests they may have asthma. If it does not, asthma will be ruled out. According to S. Hasan Arshad and K. Suresh Babu, authors of the book *The Facts: Asthma,* "an improvement in spirometry results … following treatment, is a cornerstone of the diagnosis of asthma."[5]

"How Severe Is My Asthma?"

Once a diagnosis of asthma is made, its severity can then be established. This helps medical professionals determine the best treatment for the patient. The goal of treatment is to control asthma symptoms, reduce the frequency and severity of asthma attacks, and relieve airway obstruction. Because different cases of asthma require different treatment, with the most severe cases requiring the most powerful medication, health care professionals evaluate the severity of the patient's symptoms so they can prescribe the most effective treatment. To simplify the process, the National Institutes of Health (NIH) established four stages of asthma based on the frequency of the patient's symptoms and the patient's lung function value: mild intermittent, mild persistent, moderate persistent, and severe persistent.

Mild intermittent asthma is the least severe type, where symptoms occur less than twice a week and lung function is normal between flare-ups. In mild persistent asthma, lung function also remains normal, but symptoms occur more than twice a week. In moderate persistent asthma, symptoms occur daily and lung function is below normal even between flare-ups. Symptoms in severe persistent asthma occur almost continuously and lung function is always below normal. Moderate and severe persistent asthma can greatly affect a patient's quality of life and limit their physical abilities.

Staying One Step Ahead

Treatment begins after the severity is assessed. Asthma stages, however, are not permanent. A patient's classification can go up or down depending on how well the disease is controlled. At the start of treatment, health care professionals work to lower the patient's classification using what is called the "stepwise approach" to treatment. According to asthma expert William E. Berger, "the basic concept of stepwise management is to initially prescribe long-term and quick-relief medications, based on the severity level that's one step higher than the severity level you're experiencing."[6]

For instance, patients diagnosed with mild intermittent asthma are initially treated as if they have mild persistent asthma. Those with mild persistent asthma are treated as if they have moderate persistent asthma, and so on. This approach has proven to be effective in rapidly reducing asthma symptoms. Once the patient's symptoms are controlled for at least a month, the medication is reduced, or stepped down, by one level. Patients generally remain on this stepped-down level of medication as long as it maintains control of their asthma.

Convenient Relief

There are many different medications used to treat asthma. They come in liquid, pill, or capsule form, but the most common treatment is an inhaler. An inhaler is a small handheld device that transforms a measured dose of liquid or powdered medication into a mist or a fine powder, which is then sprayed into the mouth and inhaled into the airways.

While inhalers vary, the most common ones are L-shaped and made of plastic. A small metal canister, which contains the medication, goes in at the top. There is a cap and nozzle on one end, where medication mists out when the metal canister is pressed down. Sometimes a clear plastic cylinder called a spacer is attached at the nozzle for children. This holds the medication before it is inhaled, which makes it easier for young children to get the full dose.

Inhalers are small and fairly easy to use, and they fit easily into pockets, purses, and backpacks. Additionally, because they deliver a high concentration of medication directly into the airways, less medicine is needed to provide immediate relief.

Young children can attach a spacer such as the one shown here to their inhaler to help them use the inhaler properly.

Although an inhaler is relatively easy to use, individuals must be able to hold the inhaler, release the spray, and inhale the medication all at the same time. Young children and the elderly may have difficulty coordinating all three steps properly. Additionally, sometimes more medication than an inhaler can provide is required in a severe asthma attack. In these cases, a nebulizer can be used instead.

A nebulizer creates an easy-to-inhale mist of a bronchodilator (the medical term for asthma rescue medicine), which a patient then inhales into their airways through a face mask or mouthpiece that is connected to the nebulizer by plastic tubing. Using a nebulizer requires very little effort from the patient. This is important in a severe attack, as a breathless asthmatic may not be able to inhale the entire dose of an inhaler effectively.

Nebulizers come in different sizes and can be powered by electricity or batteries. Treatment delivered with a nebulizer or inhaler generally takes effect in about 5 to 15 minutes.

A nebulizer is a little more complicated than an inhaler, so the best way for a child to receive their treatment is with the help of a parent or guardian.

Short-Term Medicine

There are two types of asthma medication: quick relief, or rescue medicine, and preventive medicine. Both are generally delivered via an inhaler or nebulizer, and both are important in managing asthma.

Quick-relief medications, which are also known as short-acting bronchodilators, are rescue drugs that are used to provide fast, temporary relief from asthma symptoms. They help stop asthma attacks after the symptoms start or prevent them from happening at all. For instance, some people use an inhaler before they exercise. Short-acting bronchodilators are not taken on a set schedule; they are taken on an as-needed basis.

There are different classes of drugs that serve as bronchodilators. Those most commonly prescribed for asthma are called beta-agonists. Beta-agonists work like adrenaline, a chemical the body produces naturally in times of crisis. Beta-agonists help the body respond quickly to an emergency by raising the patient's heart rate and blood pressure and relaxing the airways. Chemicals in these drugs attach to and stimulate cells called beta-receptors located in the small muscles surrounding the airways. Stimulating beta-receptors causes the swollen muscles in the airway to relax and open, allowing the person to breathe more easily.

The most commonly prescribed short-acting bronchodilator is called albuterol. Some over-the-counter (OTC) inhalers use different medications; these are cheaper but have more dangerous side effects and do not work as well as albuterol. Common side effects of OTC inhalers include vomiting, dizziness, shakiness, sinus pain, and difficulty sleeping. Although more uncommon, some people have reported chest pain, increased blood pressure, and coughing up blood when they use the OTC medication Asthmanefrin and its EZ Breathe atomizer, prompting the Food and Drug Administration (FDA) to issue safety concerns about this product. Medical professionals generally recommend OTC inhalers only for people who rarely need to use them, although many believe they should not be used at all.

Short-acting bronchodilators are fast acting. They take effect in about five minutes and keep working for 2 to 4 hours. Although they open the airways, they have no effect on the underlying inflammation. In addition, bronchodilators, like any other drug, can cause negative side effects. These include high blood pressure, muscle cramps, nervousness, and restlessness. However, because quick-relief medication can save an asthmatic's life, the benefit of the medication generally outweighs the health risks. People with asthma are advised to carry an inhaler containing rescue medicine with them at all times. Athletes should carry their rescue medicine on them while playing sports rather than leaving it on the sidelines. The Allergy and Asthma Network gave an example:

> One teen athlete from Nevada, who signed up as a soccer player, knew he was allergic to several kinds of pollen, including sage brush. He played soccer during the late summer and early fall, when all kinds of pollen were being released into the air.
>
> His father (coach) was not always able to help him control his allergy attacks, so he realized he needed to take control of his symptoms himself. Shortly after this, his parents helped him modify the actuator (the plastic housing the medication canister) so he could wear it on a string around his neck and treat his symptoms himself as needed.[7]

Having immediate access to the drug is so vital that most schools require nurses to have asthma medication readily available rather than locked up, the way most other medications are. According to the American Lung Association, "self-carry" asthma rescue medicine laws have been passed in all 50 states and the District of Columbia, and all that is generally required is a signed note from both the student's parent or guardian and doctor. These laws permit students with asthma to carry their inhalers with them at all times and to self-administer the medication as needed. Time and lives are saved by having medication so readily available, as a student does not have to obtain their medication from a nurse first. However, the association also reported that some individual school policies create barriers that prevent students from accessing their medication, which can be fatal:

> *Between 1990 and 2003, 38 asthma-related deaths in schools were reported. One study found that over 60 percent of asthma deaths in children came from a sudden asthma attack, rather than from the gradual worsening of symptoms. Sudden attacks can be fatal within an hour. For a child who is struggling to breathe, the trip from the classroom or the playing field to the school health room for medication can be perilously [dangerously] far.*[8]

In 2014, the American Lung Association sent out an assessment to schools to get a clearer picture of how self-carry laws are being interpreted. It found that 4 percent of respondents said their school had no such policy, while another 4 percent were unsure of whether or not there was a policy. Even in schools that had a self-carry policy, some barriers existed. For instance, some parents do not like having to provide authorization to the school, which is required to make sure students are not abusing medication. Some state laws address this by specifically stating the school cannot be held responsible for any problems that come from a child self-carrying their medication. Another issue was that some schools restrict students' access to their medication as a punishment, a practice the American Lung Association called "dangerous for the student and counter to the goal of empowering them to manage their own health."[9] So although laws that help students with asthma are in place, there is more work to be done in the way the laws are interpreted and followed. The association created guidelines a school must follow in order to consider itself asthma-friendly:

- *Identify and monitor all students with a diagnosis of asthma.*

- *Obtain individualized Asthma Action Plans for all students with asthma to monitor and manage symptoms and reduce exposure to potential asthma triggers.*

- *Establish well-communicated, step-by-step standard emergency protocols for students without Asthma Action Plans as well as undiagnosed students with respiratory distress.*

- *Educate all school personnel (especially health service professionals, teachers, physical education teachers, and coaches) about asthma, including how to handle an asthma emergency.*

- *Provide a full-time registered nurse in every school, every day, all day.*

- *Ensure students with asthma know the policies and procedures to self-carry, self-administer and have access to quick relief medications (i.e., albuterol inhaler).*

- *Ensure that students whose asthma is not well controlled are provided with self-management education and case management.*[10]

Long-Term Medicine

Unlike quick-relief medicine, preventive or long-term control medicine is taken regularly even when patients do not have any asthma symptoms. Preventive medications are anti-inflammatory drugs, which means they interfere with the immune system by reducing the chronic inflammation seen in asthma sufferers. By controlling inflammation, preventive medicine reduces the possibility of an asthma flare-up, but it has no effect on the airways once an attack is in progress.

There are a number of different preventive medicines. The most popular are corticosteroids. Corticosteroids get their name from cortisol; they are synthetic, or man-made, copies of inflammation-fighting hormones found in the human body. Corticosteroids are powerful drugs that suppress the immune system. When taken in pill form, they suppress the immune system's response in the entire body, which can increase a person's risk for illnesses such as the flu because it is harder for the immune system to fight off invading germs. However, when inhaled, corticosteroids suppress only the immune system in the lungs and do not generally increase the risk of other types of illness unless the dose is very high. By doing this, they decrease swelling, mucus production, and hyper-responsiveness in the airways. Since the drug helps keep the airways open, consistent use of preventive medication reduces the severity of attacks when they occur.

Unlike rescue medicine, preventive medicine does not work immediately. Instead, it must build up in an individual's bloodstream before taking effect. Patients must use the medication consistently for 1 to 3 weeks before they see any improvement in their symptoms. While some may be tempted to reduce their dosage once symptoms lessen or stop, this is not a good idea. Doing so can lessen the protective effect of the medicine, and stopping its use entirely can actually increase the severity of asthma symptoms and attacks. Author and asthma expert Thomas F. Plaut explained,

"When it rains, an umbrella can keep you dry. Do you close it while it is still raining? No. You will get wet. Asthma 'control' medicines work like an umbrella. They protect you from asthma symptoms and episodes. Symptoms often return when you stop taking long-term control medicine."[11]

Because preventive asthma medicine is inhaled, only small amounts enter the bloodstream. Therefore, the medication does not present the same health risk as ingested or injected steroids, which can weaken the bones and muscles as well as damage the heart. However, if a person uses the inhaler incorrectly and corticosteroids are sprayed onto the throat instead of the airways, steroids can build up in the throat until a fungus forms. This can cause an unpleasant fungal infection known as thrush, which causes a sore throat. Experts say this can generally be prevented if the person rinses their mouth and throat with water after inhaling corticosteroids.

By reducing asthma symptoms, long-term control medicine can greatly improve asthma sufferers' quality of life. "I take my medicine every day," said Julia, a young woman who has asthma. "Since I started using it every day, I have not had an asthma attack. It's been a couple of years. I don't like taking medicine, but I am afraid not to take my preventive medicine. It has really helped me."[12]

The SMART Study

Sometimes corticosteroids are not enough to control a person's asthma symptoms, especially in cases of severe persistent asthma. In these cases, corticosteroids are combined with another drug: long-acting bronchodilators. Some drug manufacturers have combined the two medications in one inhaler to make it easier for patients who need them. Over time, the combination of the two medications has been known

Are Alternative Treatments Safe?

Alternative treatments are treatments that are not widely accepted by the traditional medical community in the United States. Unlike conventional treatments, alternative treatments are not subject to rigorous testing and careful regulation by the FDA. Some treatments are harmless, although they may not be effective. Others have been found to be fake and even dangerous.

Acupuncture is one popular alternative treatment for asthma. Acupuncturists insert hair-thin needles into specific points in the patient's body in an effort to open the flow of energy within the body. This, acupuncturists say, helps the immune system function better, resulting in easier breathing through decreased mucus production and relaxed airways. According to registered respiratory therapist John Bottrell,

> One study showed that 70% of those who tried acupuncture experienced improved asthma. However, the general consensus of the medical community is that studies are inconclusive and fail to show how it works, which is why it remains an alternative asthma remedy in most of the world. To say studies are inconclusive by no means verifies that it does not work, it simply means that more studies are needed to convince the medical community.[1]

In 2012, Americans spent an estimated $30 billion on alternative medicine and treatments—many of which were falsely advertised and had no science-based research to back up their claims. For example, there is a myth that having a Chihuahua in the house or lying on a person's chest will cure asthma, although there is no proof that this is true. It is important to speak with a health professional before beginning

Acupuncture, like all alternative remedies, should be discussed with a doctor before it is tried.

any type of alternative treatment to avoid taking health risks. Bottrell advised "talking to your asthma doctor before trying alternative remedies. That said ... it only makes sense to keep your mind open for anything that might help you obtain ideal asthma control."[2] As long as an alternative remedy is not harmful to the patient or overly expensive, a doctor may approve it.

1. John Bottrell, "8 Non-Traditional Asthma Treatments," Asthma.net, July 12, 2017. asthma.net/living/8-non-traditional-asthma-treatments.

2. Bottrell, "8 Non-Traditional Asthma Treatments."

to control and maintain asthma symptoms so well that some patients can step down and discontinue the long-acting bronchodilator. Long-acting bronchodilators work the same way short-acting bronchodilators do. They relax and open the muscles surrounding the airways, but rather than having an immediate effect, long-acting bronchodilators take at least 30 minutes to take effect and last for 12 hours, so they are inhaled twice a day.

Long-acting bronchodilators are not without risk. The medicine has been associated with severe asthma attacks and asthma deaths, especially when the drug is taken without an inhaled steroid. In 2006, a 28-week U.S. study known as the Salmeterol Multicenter Asthma Research Trial (SMART) compared the safety of a long-acting bronchodilator called Salmeterol on 13,176 asthmatics to that of a placebo, or fake remedy, on an equal number of asthmatics. Subjects in both groups who used inhaled steroid medication before entering the study continued to do so. However, the researchers observed that daily use of Salmeterol correlated with more asthma attacks and more hospital visits compared to those receiving the placebo. Furthermore, there were 13 asthma-related deaths among the subjects using the long-acting bronchodilator, compared to 3 asthma-related deaths in the placebo group.

Because of these findings, in 2010, the FDA required that manufacturers of long-acting bronchodilators place a warning on the package that alerts patients not to use the drug without inhaled steroids. It also alerts them to the fact that long-acting bronchodilators have been linked to potential safety risks, but the risk is not strong enough to remove the drug from the market. A doctor and a patient should work together to make an informed decision before beginning long-acting bronchodilator treatment. It is for short-term help, to be used only until severe asthma symptoms are better controlled.

A New Hope

In March 2017, the University of Leicester reported finding a protein called HMGB1 that is linked to the narrowing of the airways in people with asthma. The hope is that someday soon, medications can be manufactured that target HMGB1 to reduce airway swelling during a severe asthma attack. Like any new medical breakthrough, however, more testing and research need to be carried out before anything is approved. Safety and effectiveness are some of the highest concerns in approving any new medical treatment—and even then, there is absolutely no guarantee that this new treatment will be 100 percent effective.

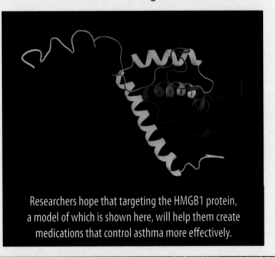

Researchers hope that targeting the HMGB1 protein, a model of which is shown here, will help them create medications that control asthma more effectively.

According to Nancy Sander, founder and president of the Allergy & Asthma Network Mothers of Asthmatics (AANMA):

> *No one with asthma should need to use a long- or short-acting bronchodilator every day for the rest of their lives if they have addressed the underlying cause of symptoms … Getting and keeping asthma under control requires a strategic plan and a clear understanding of the role of allergies … and other contributing factors.*[13]

In other words, control is the goal. While asthma attacks are sometimes unavoidable, someone whose asthma is well controlled should not have to use a rescue inhaler more than twice a week, according to guidelines from the NIH. However, it may take several years to achieve that control.

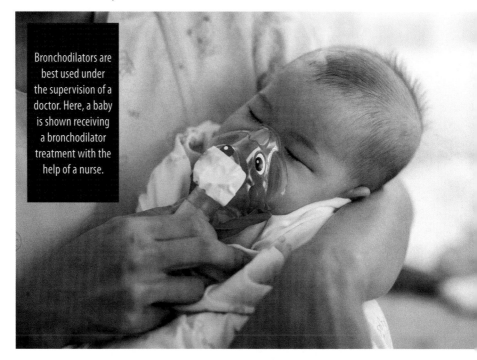

Bronchodilators are best used under the supervision of a doctor. Here, a baby is shown receiving a bronchodilator treatment with the help of a nurse.

All medications have side effects, and asthma medications are no different. However, despite the risks that some asthma medications carry, most health care professionals and people with asthma agree that effectively using rescue and preventive medications is a major step in controlling asthma symptoms.

CHAPTER THREE

AVOIDING ASTHMA TRIGGERS

Taking medication is not the only thing people with asthma can do to control their illness. Identifying and avoiding their individual triggers, which vary from person to person, is an important way to reduce the need for rescue medication. Not all triggers are easily avoidable. For instance, some stores allow pets, so someone whose asthma is set off by pet dander may unknowingly walk into one of these stores. However, in many cases, avoiding triggers can be achieved by taking precautions such as asking certain questions and doing research online.

Trying an Asthma Diary

According to Berger:

> *Avoidance seems simple enough. In real life, however, the trick is figuring out—short of living in a bubble—the practical and effective steps you can take to minimize your contact with triggers. Environmental control measures are vital components of any ... treatment plan. Every practicing allergist [a doctor who treats allergies and allergy-related asthma] focuses on helping you create and implement an effective avoidance strategy for you, your spouse, your child, or other people with asthma who live with you.[14]*

The first step in creating this type of plan is identifying what substances, events, or factors trigger an individual's symptoms. Once this is known, people can take steps to avoid or limit their exposure to these triggers. When this is not possible, they can take medication. Someone who encounters a trigger in their daily life, such as at work, may need a long-acting bronchodilator, while someone who can avoid their triggers most of the time may need only asthma rescue medication before and after being exposed to the triggers.

Since most individuals with asthma are sensitive to multiple triggers, identifying all of them is not easy. Keeping an asthma diary can help. In it, individuals record how they feel every day. They note their general health, asthma symptoms, and emotional state. They include specific information such as where they went, what the weather was, who they were with, what activities they participated in, and what, if any, effect these factors had on their asthma symptoms. Individuals and health care professionals use this information to analyze what factors improve or worsen a patient's asthma symptoms and to pinpoint specific triggers. For instance, if patients note that they cough and wheeze on cold days, this likely indicates that their airways are sensitive to cold air. Knowing this, they can then take steps to minimize their exposure to cold air. In this manner, individuals gain more control over their asthma.

How Skin Can Help

If patients note in their asthma diary that their symptoms are seasonal or that they worsen when they are outdoors, it is likely that allergens trigger their symptoms. Symptoms can also be triggered by exposure to dust, mold, or pets. Most people with allergies are sensitive to multiple substances, and undergoing an allergy test helps identify exactly which allergens trigger asthma symptoms in affected individuals.

Checking the Air Quality

Many people with asthma are sensitive to pollen. Checking the daily pollen count and taking steps to limit outdoor activities when pollen counts are high can help individuals who are sensitive to pollen manage their symptoms. If someone has their phone's location turned on, simply googling "pollen count for today" will display the count wherever they are. It is a measurement of the total number of pollen grains found in each cubic meter of air. The count is for all types of pollen and is not generally broken down into particle types.

Trees and other plants produce pollen. The more they produce, the higher the pollen count is.

Pollen counts fall into five categories: no pollen; low, or 1 to 10 pollen grains per cubic meter; moderate, or 11 to 50 pollen grains per cubic meter; high, or 51 to 500 pollen grains per cubic meter; and very high, or more than 500 pollen grains per cubic meter. Most people with asthma who are sensitive to pollen experience asthma symptoms on high and very high pollen days. Moderate and low days tend to affect only the most sensitive individuals.

The most common test is called a skin prick or scratch test. It involves exposing the skin to different allergens and then observing the body's reaction. During the test, a health care professional applies small drops of diluted extracts of different allergens to tiny scratches on the patient's forearm or back. As many as 40 allergens—such as tree pollen, dust, mold, and pet dander—may be applied during one test.

If the patient is sensitive to a particular allergen, the skin where the allergen was applied will become red and swollen. This indicates that inflammation is present, which means the body is having an allergic reaction to the particular allergen. This does not prove that the allergen is an asthma trigger, but in most cases, when an asthmatic's skin is sensitive to a particular allergen, so are their airways.

Retired professional football player Chad Brown knows the importance of getting asthma diagnosed. He once said,

> *I was actually happy when I was diagnosed with asthma, because it gave me answers to questions that had been plaguing me for over a year. And by getting treatment I am completely able to control my condition. It hasn't prevented me or stopped me from doing anything. It has actually, by being discovered, helped me to prolong my career and play the way that I play.*[15]

Allergy-Proofing a Home

Once individuals know their allergen or non-allergen triggers, they can take steps to minimize their exposure to them. Many asthma triggers, such as dust mites, mold, cockroach droppings, mice, secondhand smoke, and cleaning chemical fumes can be found in everyday homes. Dust mites in particular are one of the most common of all asthma triggers.

Dust mites are microscopic, spider-like creatures that thrive in any dark, warm, moist environment. They live in dust, feeding on the dead skin flakes that humans shed. People shed a lot of dead skin as they sleep, so bedrooms are the most popular home for dust mites. In fact, the average mattress contains about 2 million dust mites. As much as 10 percent of the weight of an old pillow is made up of living and dead dust mites, their droppings, and human skin. This is just one reason why many asthma symptoms worsen at night. Dust mites can also be found on stuffed toys, upholstered furniture, rugs, and curtains.

It is impossible to totally avoid the little creatures, but individuals can reduce their exposure to them by encasing their bedding in special covers that repel dust mites. They can wash their bedding and stuffed toys in hot water, as well as put stuffed toys in the freezer for about 5 hours each week to kill the mites. Some people keep stuffed toys off their beds and use an air conditioner or a dehumidifier to dry out household air, since dry air in the home makes it more difficult for dust mites to survive.

Vacuuming carpets and cloth-covered furniture with a vacuum that has a high efficiency particle arrester (HEPA) filter also helps. HEPA filters can help remove tiny particles, such as dust mites, from the home. According to Berger, "HEPA filters absorb and contain 99.97 percent of all particles larger than 0.3 microns (1/300 the width of a human hair) ... HEPA filters are vital tools for desensitizing and allergy proofing your indoor environment."[16] However, since any vacuum briefly increases the amount of dust mites in the air, it is best if someone who does not have asthma does the vacuuming. People with asthma should leave the room while this is done.

According to the website KidsHealth, "It's important to learn how to control the triggers in your house. This is especially important in rooms where you spend a lot of time, like your bedroom."[17] So, in an effort

Dust mites can be found all around the house, but luckily, there are steps people can take to reduce their exposure to them.

to completely dislodge dust mites, some people with asthma get rid of all curtains, soft upholstered furniture, and rugs. They generally replace them with roll shades or mini-blinds; leather, vinyl, or wood furniture; and hard flooring.

Mold Sensitivity

Mold is another common household asthma trigger that is often linked to carpeting. Like dust mites, mold needs humidity to flourish. If carpets get wet, the padding underneath can develop and retain mold. It also thrives in bathrooms, laundry areas, basements, attics, refrigerators, houseplants, garbage cans, and other damp parts of the house. Mold is found outdoors as well. The spores typically increase on humid, rainy, and foggy days and can get into the house through open windows, doors, and vents.

A 2010 study that examined the effect of mold on children with asthma in New Orleans, Louisiana, after Hurricane Katrina found a rise in asthma symptoms among children because of the increased concentration of mold throughout the city. Researcher Floyd Malveaux explained:

> The mold concentration increased tremendously— in homes and throughout the indoor and outdoor environment. Many children left the area ... Those who did stay, we worked with them and tested them. We found about 78 percent of those who had asthma were sensitive to mold ... If you're in an environment that's quite humid like New Orleans, there is already a lot of mold in the air. With the flooding, when there was up to eight to ten feet of water, you're creating a very moist environment. It becomes a big soup, where microorganisms grow. The mold remains in the walls, carpeting, and just takes over the entire environment.[18]

Keeping humidity below 50 percent in the home helps reduce mold. Using an air purifier with a HEPA filter also helps. An air purifier is a machine that helps clean indoor air and can filter out mold and other irritants. Getting rid of houseplants can help, too, as soil can harbor mold. Cleaning damp areas such as bathrooms, washing machines, trash cans, walls, floors, and ceilings with bleach or other mold-killing substances also helps. However, chemicals and scents in household cleaners also trigger asthma symptoms in some individuals. For this reason, many people with asthma create more natural cleaners, combining baking soda, vinegar, or lemon juice with water. They also use unscented detergents, soaps, and beauty products. This greatly reduces irritating fumes and possible triggers.

Minimizing Other Triggers

Other household triggers can also be minimized with a little effort. Exposure to secondhand smoke can be eliminated when people with asthma ban smoking from their homes. This means family members who smoke either have to give up smoking or go outside when they want a cigarette. Breathing in cigarette smoke has negative side effects for everyone, which is why many public buildings have rules about how far away from the door smokers must stand. When smokers do not follow those rules, people are often forced to walk through a cloud of smoke, which can be especially dangerous for those with asthma. The chemicals in smoke are known to stick to clothes and other fabrics, allowing it to be carried anywhere. Smoke from fireplaces and wood stoves can also be a problem for sensitive individuals.

Other triggers, such as cockroach droppings, may be harder to control. The bugs are a particular problem in urban areas, where people live in apartments where the creatures can move freely through the connecting walls. This is especially true in the South, where cockroaches thrive in the warmth; according to CNN, nine of the top ten roach-infested cities are in the South, although the bugs are not uncommon in the North. A survey by the Census Bureau found that 41 percent of homes in New Orleans have cockroaches—the highest concentration in the United States.

To minimize cockroach droppings, asthma patients are advised to keep their kitchens free of crumbs and wash out pet bowls and dirty dishes. Many individuals hire a pest control professional to destroy cockroaches in their home. As a final step, they seal cracks in their walls to eliminate cockroach entry points. Sealing holes and cracks also helps minimize infestations of mice, whose droppings can also trigger asthma symptoms.

Life with Pets

Other nonhuman household members are more welcome. Many households include pets, and although they are often beloved family members, they trigger asthma symptoms in about 30 percent of asthmatics. Even though giving up a pet can be very difficult, many people with asthma do this to lessen their asthma symptoms. One woman named Rachel Aydt gave her cat away when she learned cat dander was triggering the asthma symptoms of her young son, Jamie. "After a trip to the emergency room we made the agonizing decision to send Charlie [the cat] away. To date, this is the biggest parental sacrifice I've ever made ... For Jamie, sacrificing his breathing wasn't an option,"[19] she said.

Asthmatics who choose to keep their pets often keep them outdoors as much as possible. When they are allowed indoors, they sometimes are kept in a restricted area. That is what Julia, whose asthma is triggered by cat dander, did with her cat. She explained, "I kept him out of my bedroom and off all the furniture. It didn't keep me from having problems, but it helped somewhat."[20]

Some people with asthma alter their social life in order to minimize their exposure to animal dander. They avoid visiting friends and family members who have pets, opting to meet somewhere else instead, which is what Matt does. He explained,

> *If I spend any more than 10-15 minutes in a house with even one cat ... I need to use my rescue inhaler 3 to 4 times as often as I usually do ... It becomes a social issue at some point ... I've inadvertently [accidentally] hurt feelings because of [animals]. I don't get asked to friends' houses who I've told about the problem. Now, I still have a great social life with many friends, but we go out, or they come to my house.*[21]

People who have both a pet and a friend or relative with asthma should remember that the person with asthma most likely does not dislike their pet; they just cannot be in the same area with it, and they cannot control this reaction. Even if a pet is shut away in another room when the friend visits, their hair and

For many people, a dog or a cat is just another member of the family. For people with asthma, animals are a potential trigger and represent some difficult decisions.

dander are generally around the house and can set off an asthma attack. Making the effort to accommodate someone who cannot be around pets is one way to be a good friend.

Outdoor Triggers and Immunotherapy

Avoiding exposure to outdoor triggers—such as pollen, air pollution, and certain weather conditions—is almost impossible, but that does not mean people with asthma cannot take steps to help minimize their symptoms. People who are sensitive to pollen or air pollution can avoid outdoor activity on high pollen or ozone alert days. Staying indoors in the early morning and late afternoon hours when pollen counts are typically highest also helps. People can also keep doors and windows closed and use a clothes dryer rather than hanging wet clothes outside where they can trap pollen. Wearing a filter mask when working outdoors is another good strategy, as it helps filter out air pollution and pollens. Similarly, for those individuals whose asthma symptoms are triggered by cold, dry weather, covering the mouth and nose with a scarf helps warm and moisten the air before it enters the airways.

Even with all of these precautions, outdoor triggers are still very difficult to control. Sometimes, some asthmatics who are allergic to pollen undergo a kind of immunotherapy often called allergy shots. In this kind of immunotherapy, small amounts of whatever substance the person is allergic to are injected under the individual's skin. This can include both outdoor and indoor substances that trigger asthma in allergic individuals. At first, the allergen is highly diluted so it does not cause an allergic reaction. Each following injection contains a slightly higher dose. The goal is to gradually desensitize the immune system to the allergen so it no longer reacts when it is exposed to the substance. This has proven to help reduce allergy symptoms, which, in turn, is thought to lessen the way the airways respond to the substance. According to Plaut, "Allergy shots may reduce your response to the triggers of asthma by

Professional Athletes with Asthma

Many people have not let asthma prevent them from becoming professional athletes. Former soccer star David Beckham, former Olympic track and field star Jackie Joyner-Kersee, and former professional football player Jerome Bettis have all publicly spoken about their asthma. Joyner-Kersee noted that myths about asthma originally kept her in denial:

I was always told as a young girl that if you had asthma there was no way you could run, jump, or do the things I was doing athletically. So, I just knew it was impossible for me to have it. It took me a while to accept that I was asthmatic. It took me a while to even start taking my medication properly, to do the things that the doctor was asking me to do. I just didn't want to believe that I was an asthmatic. But once I stopped living in denial, I got my asthma under control, and I realized that it is a disease that can be controlled. But there were things I had to do to get it under control.[1]

As a child, Jackie Joyner-Kersee (shown here) was told that people with asthma cannot have successful athletic careers, but she proved that this was a myth.

1. Quoted in Kimberly Holland and Elizabeth Santoro, "Accomplished Athletes Who Have Asthma," Healthline, February 2, 2017. www.healthline.com/health/famous-athletes-with-asthma#1.

causing your body to build up its defenses against certain allergens."[22]

Balancing Exercise and Stress

Emotionally charged or stressful situations are also difficult to completely avoid. People whose asthma is triggered by emotional factors try to limit their exposure to stressful situations as much as possible by avoiding activities and people that cause them stress.

Exercise can trigger asthma symptoms in some people. However, most health care professionals encourage individuals with asthma to be physically active unless they suffer from very severe asthma. Exercise strengthens the body and gives people more energy. This is especially beneficial for people with asthma, who often suffer from fatigue caused by asthma attacks. Exercise also strengthens the heart, making it better able to deliver oxygen to the body, and it builds up the chest muscles that can be weakened by persistent asthma attacks. Exercise reduces stress, too. Physical activity stimulates the body to produce endorphins, which are natural chemicals that give individuals a feeling of well-being.

Less stress means fewer stress-related asthma symptoms, so exercise is very important. In addition, there is growing evidence that exercise calms the immune system, allowing the body to suppress the production of chemicals that cause inflammation. Former professional football player Keenan Burton, who was diagnosed with asthma when he was nine years old, believes that staying active has helped strengthen his body and has made it easier to keep his symptoms under control. "The reason why my asthma is not bad now is because of all the exercising and staying in shape in the past," he explained. "The more active you are, the better the chance of overcoming it."[23]

Rather than give up exercise, people with exercise-induced bronchoconstriction (EIB)—previously known as exercise-induced asthma—take other steps to lessen the chance of their symptoms arising. Exercise can narrow airways in people with EIB in just a matter of minutes. Therefore, to help prevent an asthma attack, health care professionals advise susceptible individuals to inhale a dose of their quick-relief bronchodilator before they begin exercising. This keeps the airways from narrowing while the individual exercises. Additionally, individuals with EIB should make a point of warming up before they start exercising. Not only does it help get the muscles ready for exercise, it also helps prepare the lungs for the stress. According to asthma expert William Silvers,

> *It's very important for kids to warm up because we know that with a slow warm-up the lungs get ready regarding the heat and water loss [reduced heat and moisture in the airways trigger EIB]. The lungs acclimate, so you don't have the rapid heat and water loss, and you don't have the sudden onset of exercise induced asthma. It takes about six minutes. The warm up is very helpful to get the lungs ready for the serious exercise.*[24]

There are also certain sports that are less likely to trigger EIB than others. Choosing activities that do not involve exposure to cold, dry air helps. Water sports, in which individuals breathe in warm, moist air, are a good option. Swimming is especially recommended because it involves controlled breathing, which strengthens the lungs.

A 2009 study at Taipei Medical University divided children with asthma into two groups. One group underwent a six-week swimming program while the other did not. At the end of the six weeks and for a year thereafter, the subjects in the swimming group experienced a reduction in asthma symptoms, emergency room visits, and school absences. The other group did not. Head researcher Wang Jeng-Shing explained, "Unlike other sports, swimming is unlikely to provoke asthma attacks. In addition to improving asthma, swimming promotes normal physical and psychological development, such as increasing lung volume, developing good breathing techniques and improving general fitness."[25]

The combination of physical activity and cold, dry air can make asthma attacks more likely.

There are still some risks people with asthma take when they exercise. For instance, some athletes have reported a condition called exercise-induced laryngeal obstruction (EILO). This is a type of severe breathing attack in which an asthmatic's vocal cords tighten, creating a loud and strained breathing sound. For those who experience EILO for the first time, it can be a scary situation, and the onset of panic can even make these kinds of attacks worse.

Luckily, practice with a certain breathing technique has been shown to help. Researchers familiar with EILO recommend exhaling all of the air out of the lungs and then inhaling air through clenched teeth. In 2016 and 2017, studies were done through therapy and training sessions for athletes, and 80 percent of those athletes reported a noticeable difference in their ability to exercise comfortably.

Managing asthma triggers is not always easy to do, but these sometimes difficult decisions can improve the quality of life for many people with asthma. Whether it involves taking up swimming rather than skiing, getting allergy shots, or going through the time and expense to cut down on dust mites and mold, it can have a huge effect on improving the quality of life for a person with asthma. Making changes in their environments and lives can mean reducing asthma symptoms for those who need it most.

CHAPTER FOUR

MINIMIZING AND CONTROLLING ASTHMA ATTACKS

A sthma cannot be cured, but by following the proper steps, it can be controlled. Someone whose asthma is well controlled can do all the things someone without asthma can do, although they may have to take more things into consideration in order to avoid their triggers. Tools have been invented to help people with asthma know as far in advance as possible when they are in danger of having an attack so they have time to either minimize the attack's severity or avoid it altogether.

Peak Flow Score

People with asthma often feel like their breathing is normal when it is not. This is because most of them do not have noticeable asthma symptoms until their airways narrow significantly. In much the same manner that people with diabetes track their blood sugar with a blood glucose meter, people with asthma can check their lung function with a device known as a peak flow meter. This meter allows patients to measure how forcefully air is blown out of the lungs as well as monitor changes in their airways. It can also alert them to a potential asthma attack. Once alerted, individuals can take steps to manage their asthma before an attack gets out of control. According to Plaut,

> *Your peak flow score often drops before you or your doctor can notice any sign of asthma. Using a meter, you ... can tell if your peak flow has dropped five percent. Using a stethoscope, your doctor may not notice a change in airflow of less than 25 percent. If you check your peak flow, you can tell early that you are having a problem and how serious it is. If you start treatment right away, you can usually avoid care in the ER.*[26]

Peak flow meters are handheld tools that resemble small tubes. They are so simple to use that patients as young as five can learn to use them. When individuals blow into a peak flow meter, an indicator moves to a point on a scale between 0 and 100. Most meters divide this scale into green, yellow, and red zones. Readings in the green zone fall between 80 and 100 and indicate normal lung functions. Readings between 50 and 79 fall in the yellow or caution zone. This zone warns individuals that their airways are starting to narrow and that asthma symptoms are developing. At this point, patients can take quick-relief medicine to pre-treat their symptoms.

Consistent yellow readings indicate that individuals do not have adequate control of their asthma and need to consult with their health care professional about stepping up a level in their use of long-acting controller medication. Readings below 50 fall in the red or danger zone, signaling poor lung function and the start of a severe asthma attack. When this happens, individuals need to stop what they are doing, immediately take quick-relief medicine, and possibly seek medical attention. Using a peak flow meter also helps the patient know when it is safe to take on physically demanding challenges and when it is time to rest.

Just because a peak flow reading reads "normal" does not always mean a person with asthma will have an easy time exercising. Everyone's body works differently. As swimmer Wayne McCauley said, "After about three weeks my peak flow values were in the normal range, but I still had poor swim practices. After five weeks I finally started going above normal on the peak flow chart and my times in swim meets dropped dramatically. It is wonderful to swim and get enough air."[27]

When a patient blows into a peak flow meter such as this one, the green, yellow, and red pointers indicate how strong their breathing is.

Document Peak Flow

Many people with asthma graph their peak flow readings on a special chart designed for this purpose. It provides individuals with a clear visual guide to how well they are managing their condition. Like a peak flow meter, the tri-colored chart features green, yellow, and red zones. Plaut explained, "The graphic design displays peak flow trends at a glance. This prompts you to take action early."[28] There are many apps available for this as well, such as Wizdy Pets, Asthma Buddy, and AsthmaMD.

Before patients begin charting their readings, they establish their personal best peak flow rate.

Asthma in Pop Culture

Until the middle of the 20th century, many people believed asthma was an emotional illness that affected nervous, weak, or timid people. In the 1960s, this theory was proven wrong, and huge advancements have since been made in the diagnosis and treatment of asthma around the world. However, this idea has persisted and has sometimes influenced the way people with asthma are treated—for example, some are told the problem is all in their head—and portrayed in the media.

One movie many people with asthma have pointed out is the 1980s cult classic *The Goonies*. One of the main characters, Mikey, is shown taking too many puffs of his inhaler—an over-the-counter brand that asthmatics have noted is less effective and causes more side effects than a prescription brand—and using it incorrectly each time. Furthermore, his character plays into the outdated stereotype that asthma can be overcome with mental strength when Mikey throws away his inhaler at the end of the movie after having overcome many obstacles. Other such examples include the movie *Hitch*, in which the main character throws away his inhaler after he finds the courage to kiss the girl he likes, and *Lord of the Flies*, in which the asthmatic character Piggy is weak and frequently ignored.

This image can have negative effects on those with asthma, both directly and indirectly, by reinforcing the idea that asthma is a made-up or unserious issue that affects only those who are too mentally weak to overcome it. This can lead to dangerous situations where someone who is having an asthma attack is not given the proper medical care, as those around them falsely believe the person is looking for attention or should be able to get over it with some mental effort. As editor and author Lucienne Diver wrote, "Let's just get something straight, people with health issues have enough problems without folks trying to pull interventions to tell them it's all just mind over matter ... I've had teachers refuse to grant me passes to the nurse because they didn't take the condition seriously, kids play keep-away with my inhaler ... you name it."[1] The asthma blog *One Bad Lung* identified the larger problem with the media's portrayal:

> It may not seem like a big deal, but these [shows] are both educating children on their limits and expected lifestyle AS WELL AS educating non-asthmatics on the appropriate response and treatment of those suffering with the disease ... Instead of creating ridiculous, debilitating characters why not celebrate our fellow asthmatics who have proved they accomplish their goals[?][2]

1. Lucienne Diver, "Why I Hate *The Goonies*," *Lucienne Diver's Drivel*, October 31, 2011. luciennediver.net/2011/10/31/why-i-hate-the-goonies.

2. Asthma Boy, "Hollywood and Asthma," *One Bad Lung*, September 6, 2013. onebadlung.com/2013/09/hollywood-and-asthma.

To determine this, patients take a peak flow reading twice a day for about a week after effective stepwise therapy has their asthma symptoms under control. The highest number becomes the patient's personal best peak flow rate, and they record it on their chart. By comparing all future readings to their best peak flow rate, they can tell how well their asthma is controlled.

Making this comparison also provides individuals with additional warnings about the possibility of an asthma attack. For example, if an individual's readings are in the green zone but they show a steady decline or are quite a bit less than the patient's personal best reading, this is a good indicator that something is wrong. Individuals can then take early action to help head off a potential attack.

A Different Plan for Everyone

Having and following an asthma action plan—also called an asthma self-management plan—is another tool that helps people with asthma manage their condition and cope during an asthma attack. An asthma action plan is a written plan that patients develop with their doctor. It tells patients what triggers to avoid, the names and dosages of all their medications, when and how they should be taken, how to adjust medicines in response to different signs or symptoms, and a list of emergency contact numbers.

Every patient's plan is different. To make following the plan simple, asthma action plans are organized around peak flow reading color zones. Plans tell patients what medication, if any, they should take if they are in the green, yellow, or red zone, what symptoms to watch for in each zone, what actions to take when these symptoms arise, when to seek professional help, and when to go directly to an emergency room. In addition, most plans have a space for patients to record where all their asthma medications are kept and when their prescriptions should be refilled. According to Arshad and Babu,

> *The objective of asthma self-management is to make the patient aware of how to manage their asthma under expert guidance. The key aspects are patient education, which is provided in a structured way, and a written self-management action plan. Peak flow is monitored regularly and asthmatic individuals are made aware of their symptoms. This helps to keep their asthma under good control and to act early when deterioration of their conditions begins.*[29]

Patients are encouraged to share their asthma action plans with their families, friends, teachers, coaches, and school nurses. That way, should an asthma attack threaten or strike, everyone involved with the patient knows what steps to take. That is why Chad Brown made sure his team knew about his asthma and kept himself prepared. He realized the importance of self-management as well as following plans made with his doctor. He explained, "Asthma … shouldn't keep you on the sidelines unless your condition is very severe, if you follow your treatment protocols. You're responsible for your medications."[30] Help from others may not be immediately available in the event of an asthma attack. It is important for people with asthma to know what their medication is and how to take it.

As an individual's asthma changes, so does their action plan. Patients typically review their asthma action plans with their doctor at least once a year, and as their medications and dosages change, adjustments are made to the action plan. All of this planning may sound like hard work, but people with asthma are often willing to put in the effort to manage their symptoms. Because they work so hard on creating an asthma action plan, people with asthma are very knowledgeable about how to treat themselves. Many express frustration when they are given advice they have not asked for. Although loved ones are generally trying to be helpful when they do this, their comments are frequently not helpful at all. For example, telling someone with asthma to try a particular treatment, to improve their overall health, or to breathe a particular way during an asthma attack—such as more slowly or through pursed lips—are all things people with asthma do not need or want to hear. Asthma is not a sign of poor overall health, and there are no miraculous, effortless cures for it. As Bottrell noted, "[People tell me] I should try yoga, acupuncture, vitamins, probiotics, or salt therapy. Look, if those cured asthma, doctors would prescribe them. But they don't, because they don't work. If they did work, asthma would have been cured long ago, and we wouldn't be here."[31]

Techniques for Avoiding Illness

Avoiding illness is another way people cope with asthma attacks. Doing so helps control their symptoms, lessens the severity of asthma attacks, and makes it easier to get through an attack. Protecting the body against respiratory infections is especially vital. Respiratory infections worsen asthma symptoms and cause a prolonged decrease in lung function in people with asthma. Research has shown that germs that cause colds, coughs, and the flu cause a heightened immune response in people with asthma. This results in high levels of inflammation, leading to severe asthma attacks. In fact, respiratory infections are the most frequent cause of asthma attacks in adults. By getting an annual flu shot and practicing social distancing, which means avoiding contact with infected individuals, people with asthma lessen their chances of developing a respiratory infection.

Carol Shea-Porter, who has served several terms in Congress, has a husband and two children who have asthma. "I used to just beg people to stay away when they had a cold," she said. "Because a cold for most people is a seven-day event, but a cold for my child with asthma would become a two-month odyssey."[32]

Social distancing also involves avoiding crowded public places such as shopping malls, movie theaters, airports, and commuter trains during flu season, as well as avoiding contact with items infected people may have touched. Cold and flu viruses can linger on hard surfaces for days and can be spread through contact with contaminated items. Touching a surface that is infected with the virus and then accidentally touching one's mouth or nose will spread the virus. To be safe, it is best for people with asthma to avoid public restrooms and water fountains during flu season as well as pens provided for customers to use in stores, restaurants, and doctor's offices. A shared pen is passed to dozens of people in any given day and is an excellent carrier of respiratory viruses. By simply using their own pens, people with asthma can limit their exposure to respiratory infections and therefore their risk of a severe asthma attack.

It is nearly impossible to avoid germs and illness completely without becoming a hermit.

Some people wear masks such as these to prevent the spread of germs. However, they are not a substitute for proper hygiene, such as handwashing.

However, people can use common sense health practices to help provide a good amount of protection. Handwashing, for example, is a good way to prevent the spread of germs. Proper handwashing with soap and warm water after contact with sick people or while in public places rinses away germs. When soap and water are not available, an alcohol-based sanitizer is a good substitute. This is especially important before touching the eyes—for example, before putting in contact lenses—and before eating, drinking, or handling food. Additionally, covering the mouth and nose with the crook of the elbow rather than the hand when coughing or sneezing can help prevent the spread of germs, as people generally do not touch things with the inside of their elbows.

Summer Camps

For 40 years, the American Lung Association in California hosted a camp for children with asthma to give them a chance to have fun while developing asthma management skills. With the help of counselors and other campers, they developed plans to avoid asthma triggers, received practice and instruction on using their inhalers correctly, and learned breathing and relaxation techniques to help them handle an asthma attack without panicking. In addition, campers participated in physical activities that strengthened their lungs, such as swimming, yoga, and tai chi, as well as other fun activities, such as archery, softball, and boating—all under the supervision of medical staff.

In June 2015, the organization stopped hosting this camp, due to "changing community needs and medical advances that help children manage their disease (allowing many more children with asthma to attend non-asthma specific summer camps)."[1] However, the Consortium on Children's Asthma Camps lists about 55 asthma camps in the United States run by various organizations for those who still want to attend one.

1. "Summer Camps for Children with Asthma," American Lung Association, accessed March 12, 2018. www.lung.org/local-content/_content-items/our-initiatives/current-initiatives/summer-camps-for-children-with-asthma.html.

If people with asthma do get a respiratory infection, they are advised to seek help from their health care professional rather than trying to treat themselves. Early and aggressive medical treatment can reduce the chances that a respiratory infection will worsen asthma symptoms.

Living a Healthy Life

Maintaining a healthy lifestyle, too, lessens an individual's risk of having an asthma attack. Although having asthma is not a sign that someone is unhealthy, everyone can benefit from living as healthily as possible. A healthy lifestyle can minimize the severity of an attack, as the body will be better equipped to cope with asthma symptoms. Getting enough sleep and eating healthy foods, for instance, are two actions that strengthen the body and the immune system, which in turn helps individuals withstand an asthma attack. Certain foods that seem to reduce inflammation are especially helpful for people with asthma. These include brightly colored fruits and vegetables and foods rich in omega-3 fatty acids, such as salmon, cod, tuna, olive oil, nuts, seeds, and wheat germ.

Shown here are some foods that are believed by many to be beneficial for people who have asthma.

Brightly colored fruits and vegetables contain flavonoids, a group of more than 4,000 substances that are believed to have many health benefits, including anti-inflammatory and antioxidant properties. Antioxidants are natural substances that help protect the body against damage caused by oxidation, a process in which cells are weakened when they come in contact with oxygen molecules. Cell damage can aggravate asthma symptoms and make it harder for the body to fight off respiratory infections. A 2006 study at Cambridge University examined whether eating fresh fruit offers protection against asthma. It compared the diets of 1,100 adults, half of whom had asthma and half of whom did not. The study found that those subjects who ate the greatest quantity of fresh fruits were the least likely to have asthma.

The study went on to analyze whether eating fruit had any effect on the frequency and severity of asthma symptoms among the subjects with asthma. It found that those subjects with asthma who ate the most fruit reported fewer asthma attacks than those who ate the least. A number of other studies have come up with comparable findings. One flavonoid in particular, quercetin, which is found in apples, onions, berries, grapes, and green tea, has caught the eye of scientists around the world. It appears to inhibit the release of inflammatory chemicals that cause the airways to narrow. A number of studies have looked at the effect of quercetin on asthmatic airways. Two Brazilian studies in 2007 and 2010 treated mice with a chemical that caused their airways to become inflamed. Then, one group of mice was given quercetin, while the other group acted as a control. This means they were not given quercetin so the researchers could see the differences between the two groups. In both studies, the airways of the mice treated with quercetin were less constricted and less inflamed. There was no significant improvement in the control group.

Conversely, foods high in fat and sodium, or salt, such as fast food and processed food, appear to worsen airway inflammation. A 2010 Australian study measured markers of airway inflammation and the lung function of asthmatics before and after the subjects were fed a meal of fast-food burgers and french fries. The subjects' lung function decreased and markers of inflammation increased after eating the high-fat meal. A similar 2010 study done by the University of Alberta, Canada, concluded that eating fast food more than once a week intensifies asthma symptoms. "Fast foods contain high levels of sodium that can increase the risk for wheezing, more 'twitchy' airways and hyper-reactive lungs,"[33] said Canadian researcher Anita Kozyrskyj. Sulfites have also been pointed out as a substance that may make asthma worse. As such, some people with asthma avoid wine, dried fruits, shrimp, and bottled lemon juice.

Limiting consumption of some foods and increasing consumption of others may help minimize worsening airway inflammation. Additionally, experts say eating large meals or foods that give people gas should be avoided, as they put pressure on the diaphragm, which can trigger asthma symptoms. However, experts caution that these results are not conclusive, which means more study is needed. Some people may find relief from making these dietary changes, while others may not.

Obesity and Asthma

Eating a healthy diet also impacts a person's weight. Maintaining a healthy body weight helps people with asthma lessen the frequency and severity of asthma attacks. Obesity is a disorder in which individuals have a body mass index (BMI) greater than or equal to 30, which makes them severely overweight. BMI is a calculation that uses a person's height and weight to estimate how much body fat they have. Although it is not a perfect indication of weight in individuals—for instance, since muscle weighs more than fat, some muscular athletes register as overweight or obese on the BMI index—it is generally useful for determining weight trends in large populations. According to the American Lung Association, 11 percent of obese adults have asthma, compared to only 7 percent of adults with a body mass index (BMI) in the normal range. Researchers are not completely sure why this is, but they believe it may be a combination of putting extra pressure on the lungs and having a higher level of inflammatory chemicals in the body, which are produced in fat tissue.

To make matters worse, obesity leads to problems in determining accurate dosing of asthma medication and appears to inhibit the effect of some medications. A 2008 National Jewish Health study in Denver determined that corticosteroids are 41 percent less effective in obese and overweight people. This was backed up by other research by the American Lung Association Airways Clinical Research Centers Network (ACRC). The ACRC has also done research that found "that people suffering with both obesity and asthma more often have other medical problems that might affect asthma."[34] These include depression and obstructive sleep apnea, in which a person stops breathing while they are sleeping. This makes them wake up for a few seconds dozens or even hundreds of times a night, depending on how severe their case is. Generally, they do not realize they have woken up and they fall right back asleep, but since their body is not getting uninterrupted sleep, they are often sleepy and have low energy during the day. This interruption in breathing can also worsen asthma symptoms. Studies have shown that when obese asthmatics lose weight, they generally gain much better control of their asthma symptoms and reduce the occurrence of sleep apnea.

Staying Relaxed

Despite patients' best efforts to derail asthma attacks before they start, attacks will still occur. By staying calm during an attack, individuals can help minimize the severity of the attack and better cope with what is happening. An asthma attack can be a very frightening experience. When individuals panic, stress causes physical changes in the body, which cause the body to release inflammatory chemicals that worsen the severity of an asthma attack. In addition, when people panic, they often hyperventilate. Hyperventilating makes it harder for someone to catch their breath and get air in and out of their narrowed airways during an attack. Therefore, according to researchers Curt Cackovic and Rotimi Adigun, "Breathing training is a method of reducing panic … Several of these slow breathing techniques have been shown to benefit patients with asthma."[35]

Learning to stay calm during an asthma attack gives individuals more control. This has been deemed so important that the American Lung Association offers a special program known as Open Airways for Schools. This program teaches children with asthma how to understand and manage their asthma; it includes the relaxation skills and specific breathing exercises that help keep hyperventilation under control. There are many different relaxation exercises. A popular one involves systematically contracting and relaxing muscles throughout the body, teaching individuals how to relax their body during an asthma attack.

Visualization and meditation are two other popular relaxation techniques. Both use the mind to calm the body and reduce feelings of panic. In meditation, individuals use concentration techniques such as silently repeating a word or chant to clear the mind. This, in turn, relaxes the body and reduces stress. Research shows that levels of inflammatory chemicals the body produces as a response to stress decrease during meditation sessions, although scientists are not certain why this happens. One study suggests it may be because mindfulness and meditation actually change the brain's connections. The *Huffington Post* described the study:

> *The researchers recruited 35 stressed-out adult job-seekers, and asked half of the participants to complete an intensive three-day mindfulness meditation retreat program while the other half completed a three-day relaxation retreat program that did not have a mindfulness component.*
>
> *The participants completed brain scans before and after the programs, and also provided blood samples before the programs and after a four-month follow-up. The brain scans revealed that meditation increased functional connectivity between two brain areas that typically work in opposition: the default mode network (which is involved in mind-wandering and internal reflection) and the executive attention network (key to attention, planning and decision-making). Relaxation training, however, did not have this effect. The blood samples showed that participants who underwent the mindfulness training had lower levels of Interleukin-6, a biomarker of inflammation, than those who did the relaxation retreat.[36]*

The researchers believe the increased brain connectivity reduced stress and that the role mindfulness played in this was to make the effect last longer than relaxation alone. However, more research must be done to confirm these findings.

Visualization is similar to meditation. While practicing visualization, individuals picture something that makes them feel happy and safe, such as a favorite vacation spot or a happy event. Individuals may also envision themselves having an asthma attack without losing control. When an attack actually happens, individuals may be able to calm themselves by thinking about their positive visions and remain in a relaxed state of mind.

There is no doubt that having an asthma attack can be very scary. Although there is no way for people with asthma to completely prevent an asthma attack from occurring, they can learn ways to control it. By learning how to remain calm during an attack, maintaining a healthy lifestyle, using a peak flow meter, and planning for emergencies, individuals with asthma will be better prepared in their everyday lives.

CHAPTER FIVE

ASTHMA TODAY AND TOMORROW

Scientists, researchers, and doctors continue to investigate the causes of asthma. The knowledge they gain may eventually help prevent the development of new cases of asthma in the future. Other studies are focusing on helping people currently suffering from asthma by developing new and improved treatments for the disease.

Studies on BPA and Asthma

Research shows that if a fetus is exposed to a harmful substance in the womb, it can affect its development and create a range of health problems once the baby is born. This is because any substance that enters a pregnant woman's bloodstream is transmitted to the developing fetus through the placenta, which is a structure through which the fetus receives vital oxygen and nutrition. This means the fetus is exposed to everything that enters the mother's blood, whether by mouth, by air, or through the bloodstream. Alcohol, medications, illegal drugs, contaminated food, and various chemicals all can harm an unborn baby. This is because fetal cells are undeveloped and fragile, making the fetus especially sensitive and vulnerable to the effects of different substances.

For years, scientists have been looking at whether fetal exposure to one particular chemical, bisphenol A (BPA), can lead to the development of asthma. BPA is found in some plastic containers and in the lining of some aluminum cans. Different animal tests have shown that exposure to BPA can affect brain and sexual development in fetal mice and rats. Knowing this, scientists theorized that the chemical might also negatively impact the development of fetal airways, possibly linking it to the development of asthma. In 2010, researchers at the University of Texas Medical Branch at Galveston put this theory to the test. They added 0, 1, or 10 micrograms per milliliter doses of BPA in the drinking water of three groups of female mice before, during, and after pregnancy. According to the scientists, the largest dose of 10 micrograms per milliliter of BPA was comparable to what a human fetus might be exposed to.

Microwaving food in plastic containers that contain BPA is one way the chemical can potentially make its way into a person's body; as the plastic heats up, the BPA leaches into the food.

Four days after the mice gave birth, the babies were injected with an allergen to make them more susceptible to asthma. The researchers then measured the level of inflammatory chemicals in the lungs of all the baby mice as well as their lung function. The mice born to the mothers who were exposed to 10 micrograms of BPA developed significant signs of asthma, including high levels of inflammation and poor lung function. The other groups did not develop asthma symptoms. Since human airways may not react in exactly the same manner, the results of the study are not conclusive evidence that fetal exposure to BPA can cause asthma.

However, this link was strengthened by another study that was published in 2014. Researchers studied the urine of 398 mothers during their pregnancy and the urine of their infants after they were born. Every time the concentration of BPA in the mother's urine went up 10 times, the likelihood that the baby would wheeze went up 55 percent. It also indicated lower lung capacity, although this generally improved by the time the child turned five. BPA levels in the child's own urine did not carry a link to increased wheezing or decreased lung capacity, leading researchers to believe exposure during pregnancy is the most important factor. The results of this study did not prove that BPA causes asthma but did show that a link exists between the two. According to Dr. Adam Spanier, the study's author, this link is enough evidence for him. He said, "If my sister who's pregnant asked me for advice, I would tell her to try to minimize her BPA exposure ... I wouldn't say let's do some more research."[37]

Based on what is already known, the FDA also recommends that parents take steps to limit fetal and infant exposure to BPA, and some doctors are advising expectant mothers to avoid using products containing the chemical. According to the National Conference of State Legislatures, "Thirteen states and the District of Columbia have enacted [BPA] restrictions since 2009."[38]

In 2010, Connecticut was the first state to pass a law banning the use of the chemical. In July 2012, the FDA announced that it "would no longer allow BPA in baby bottles and children's drinking cups."[39] Many stores have removed products containing BPA, such as plastic baby bottles and pacifiers. If further studies prove that fetal exposure to BPA does, in fact, lead to the development of asthma, it is likely the chemical will be banned more widely. This may possibly lessen the prevalence of asthma cases in the future. However, BPA is still allowed in many other consumer products, which pregnant women should be aware of if they want to limit their exposure.

Possible Dangers of Acetaminophen

Another chemical, acetaminophen, has caught the interest of other researchers. Acetaminophen is a common ingredient in OTC pain, fever, and cold medicines. Because the rate of childhood asthma and the number of people using acetaminophen to treat fevers both rose dramatically after the 1980s, scientists wanted to see if there was a link between them or if it was a spurious correlation, which is the phrase used when two things seem related but are not. In 2009, scientists at Columbia University in New York studied fetal exposure to acetaminophen and its effect on the development of asthma in children. The researchers compared acetaminophen use during pregnancy in 301 women to the prevalence of asthma symptoms in their children at five years old. The mothers were surveyed about how frequently they used acetaminophen during their pregnancy, how frequently their children wheezed, and how frequently the children had visited an emergency room for respiratory problems. The researchers found that 34 percent of the mothers used acetaminophen during their pregnancy and 27 percent of their children had asthma.

The children whose mothers used acetaminophen were more likely to wheeze and were more likely to visit the emergency room for respiratory problems than the children of women who did not. Scientists also found that the risk increased as the number of days of prenatal exposure to the chemical increased. A similar study in Great Britain came up with similar results. "These findings … suggest caution in the use of acetaminophen during pregnancy,"[40] said lead researcher Matthew S. Perzanowski.

However, there were some problems with these studies. Neither one used a control group, so the researchers cannot say for sure whether taking acetaminophen actually causes asthma. Additionally, according to the AAAAI, the studies did not take into account the fact that if someone was using acetaminophen, it was because they had some illness to treat. Some researchers questioned whether the fever or its accompanying illness, rather than the medication used to treat it, was the problem. In a 2014 study that was published in *The Journal of Allergy and Clinical Immunology*, researchers investigated the link between asthma and antipyretics, or fever-reducing medications, both during pregnancy and in the first year of an infant's life. This study controlled for early life respiratory infections, which are a major reason for antipyretic use. Before applying this control, it did seem as if infants who were given more acetaminophen had an increased risk of developing asthma. However, after applying the control, "risk estimates were substantially diminished (particularly for the early childhood outcome), suggesting that underlying respiratory infections may drive the association between antipyretic intake and asthma."[41] Another study that compared the use of acetaminophen and ibuprofen, another OTC antipyretic, found that "the use of acetaminophen, as compared with ibuprofen, did not worsen asthma or wheezing in children."[42] However, this second study did not research whether acetaminophen causes asthma symptoms in otherwise healthy children. Further research is ongoing to get a clearer understanding of these issues.

Prenatal Stress

Other scientists are investigating whether a stressful pregnancy increases a baby's chances of developing asthma. Previous studies using animals have shown that prenatal stress can negatively affect the development of the fetal immune system, and in 2010, Harvard University scientists undertook a study with human participants. They questioned a total of 557 pregnant women about the amount and type of stress in their lives, including questions about financial worries, family problems, and crime in their communities. In each of the families surveyed, one of the parents had asthma or allergies. As a result, each of the babies had a similar, but not exact, genetic risk of developing asthma.

When the babies were born, the scientists took umbilical cord blood samples, which they tested with different allergens. The babies born to the mothers who reported being under the most stress produced the highest level of an inflammatory chemical associated with airway constriction and asthma. In comparison, babies born to the least stressed mothers produced very low levels of the chemical. Lead researcher Rosalind Wright explained:

> *This is the first human study to corroborate [support] research from animal studies demonstrating that stress experienced by mothers during pregnancy influences the child's developing immune system starting in the womb ... The cytokine [inflammatory chemical] patterns seen in the higher-stress groups, an indicator of how the child's immune system is functioning at birth and responding to the environment, may be a marker of increased risk for developing asthma as they get older.*[43]

Stress is a normal part of life, but it can be unhealthy over long periods of time. For pregnant women, stress can sometimes affect their unborn child.

In a follow-up study in 2016, the researchers studied the effect of prenatal stress on these children, who at the time were six years old. They concluded, "While boys were more vulnerable to stress during the prenatal period, girls were more impacted by postnatal stress and cumulative stress across both periods in relation to asthma."[44] They found that the children's first two years were the most important and that stress at home and in their environment had the largest effect on the girls by the time the participants reached the age of six. These girls were more likely to have developed asthma than the boys.

Studies on Air Pollution

Scientists are continuing to look at environmental factors that may cause asthma, such as air pollution. Scientists already know that air pollution can irritate the airways of people with and without asthma and that asthma is widespread in inner cities, where air pollution is generally greatest. Based on these factors, a number of scientists have been investigating whether exposure to high levels of air pollution may actually cause asthma to develop in children. Children are the focus of these studies because their lungs are still developing and are therefore more vulnerable to harmful chemicals than adults' lungs.

The Children's Health Study, which was sponsored by the California Air Resources Board, was a long-term study that took place from 1992 to about 2004. It monitored the lung function and the frequency of respiratory problems of 5,500 school-age children. These children lived in 12 different communities in Southern California. Depending on which community they lived in, the children were exposed to varying levels of air pollution on a daily basis. The scientists measured concentrations of different pollutants that the children were exposed to and compared this data to the children's lung function rates. They also looked at the frequency of any respiratory problems they had.

The scientists found that the children living in the communities with the highest levels of pollution were three to five times more likely to have below-normal lung function rates than the children living in communities with lower levels of pollution. They also found that new cases of asthma were most likely to occur among the children who were exposed to high levels of ozone, a substance that is created when exhaust fumes from cars and trucks are exposed to sunlight.

Rates were highest among those children who played sports outdoors in high-ozone areas. In fact, young athletes in the high-ozone communities were three times more likely to develop asthma than their peers in low-ozone communities. The scientists hypothesized that the airways of young athletes are especially vulnerable to ozone because athletes generally breathe deeply and rapidly while they are exercising, causing them to inhale about 20 times more pollutants than non-athletes. In 2016, the researchers received a grant of $45 million from the NIH to continue their research. This phase is expected to last seven years and will look at how pollution from freeways affects fetuses. The researchers recruited more than 750 pregnant women in the Los Angeles, California, area who will be studied to see how the pollution they breathe in affects their child's risk of developing asthma.

Swedish researchers have also looked for a link between traffic pollution and the development of asthma. In 2008, they monitored 4,000 infants and children who were no more than a year old. Some lived in the city and some lived in the countryside, allowing the researchers to see how different levels of exposure to traffic pollution affected the subjects' chances of developing asthma symptoms. The scientists found that the subjects who were exposed to the highest levels of traffic fumes were 60 percent more likely to have persistent asthma symptoms than the subjects who were not exposed to the pollution. A 2018 study from the University of Leeds in England found similar results when they looked at the British city of Bradford, concluding that up to 38 percent of asthma cases in children who lived there may have been caused by air pollution.

Reducing pollution is one reason many people have pushed for a switch from fossil fuels, such as gas, coal, and oil, to clean energy. They support actions such as passing laws that limit the amount of different pollutants factories and motor vehicles emit, requiring motor vehicles to produce fewer carbon emissions, and sponsoring research into the development of clean fuel. However, these measures will take quite a while to have an effect. Some people have taken more immediate action to lower asthma rates, such as building schools and parks far from high traffic areas. Some schools are prohibiting cars and school buses from leaving their engines running as they pick up and drop off students on school grounds. When cars and school buses leave their engines running while they wait for students, it increases air pollution around the school. Dangerous particles also get inside the buses and into classrooms through vents and open windows. In an article for the Georgia news outlet *Savannah Now*, experts noted,

A line of idling school buses doesn't just pollute the air around the buses. They also pollute the air in the bus and can emit particulates that can enter the school, reducing the air quality inside too ... It takes individual, family, and community action to change these practices. Each person taking baby steps will add up. If every parent waiting in line to pick up their children turns their car off, it helps.[45]

Solar panels and wind turbines can power cities cleanly, compared to power plants that burn coal or gas for electricity. Clean energy can decrease the air pollution that makes asthma symptoms worse.

Such efforts, if used widely, may help reduce future asthma cases. In the meantime, some experts advise families with young children to avoid living close to freeways and major roads. Furthermore, those with asthma should look closely at their local weather forecasts before playing or exercising outside. On days when the ozone levels are high, it is best for people with asthma to remain indoors.

Taking Action

In February 2018, King's College in London reported that the city's maximum pollution levels for the entire year had been surpassed in just one month. Vehicles, factories, home heating and cooling systems, and many other things people use every day are contributing to pollution around the world, and this polluted air gets around through windows, air conditioners, and vents. This, in turn, means that people with asthma can be affected by pollution in what should be the safety of their own homes.

Some governments are fighting air pollution by passing laws requiring power to come from clean energy sources, such as solar, wind, and water. Clean energy means the source does not release carbon dioxide or other chemicals into the air. Less air pollution means fewer asthma attacks, which in turn means fewer visits to the hospital and doctors' offic-

Smog dangerously covers cities such as Hong Kong (shown here). Bigger cities tend to have more vehicles and more factories, leading to higher levels of smog.

es. In the United Kingdom (UK), there is a government program called T-Charge that charges a fee to the drivers of older, heavy-emission vehicles in an effort to encourage the switch to newer and cleaner cars.

In 1963, the Clean Air Act was established in the United States to fight pollution, and major amendments were made to it in 1970 and 1990. It is important to watch for any changes that could be made to this act. Even a slight change in regulations and laws for corporations and factories could mean a higher chance of dangerous chemicals and fumes ending up in the air.

Promising New Treatments

While some scientists are investigating possible causes of asthma to prevent new cases from developing, others are working on developing new and better treatments to help people today. One newer treatment is aimed at helping people with severe persistent asthma. While current asthma medications help most people, it is harder to get severe asthma symptoms under control. As a result, people with severe persistent asthma take stronger and more frequent doses of asthma medication than people with less severe asthma. This increases their risk of experiencing harmful side effects. A treatment known as bronchial thermoplasty helps people with severe persistent asthma gain better control of their symptoms.

Bronchial thermoplasty involves using radio waves to heat the muscle walls that surround the airways in the lungs. People with severe asthma often have too much smooth muscle in their airways; the heat removes this extra muscle, making the airways less constricted. Less constriction, of course, means easier breathing. During this procedure, a tiny tube attached to a device known as a bronchoscope is passed through the patient's mouth or nose into the airways. A camera on the bronchoscope allows the doctor to see inside via a computer screen. The tip of the tube delivers radio waves to the muscles surrounding the airways. The radio waves are about the same temperature as a warm cup of coffee, which is hot enough to cause the muscles to relax without burning or scarring them. The procedure is performed over three hour-long sessions. The patient's airways are numbed before each session to minimize any discomfort.

A clinical trial (a test using human subjects) was done on 297 severe asthma patients in 2010.

Patients in the trial showed a 32 percent reduction in asthma attacks and an 84 percent decrease in emergency room visits. In fact, the trial was so successful that the FDA approved the use of bronchial thermoplasty that same year. Other studies have found similar results. According to Boston Scientific, a company that makes the medical equipment used in the bronchial thermoplasty procedure, the treatment reduces asthma attacks for at least 5 years. However, it is currently available only for severe persistent asthma patients who are 18 or older whose asthma cannot be controlled through other methods.

Another treatment method for severe asthma, which is in clinical trials as of 2018, is called targeted lung denervation (TLD). According to Dr. Nick ten Hacken, one of the lead researchers, "TLD is the first medical procedure that targets the whole lung by disrupting the overactive nerves into the lungs, thereby opening up the airways and making it easier to breathe."[46] The one-hour procedure is done by using a bronchoscope to insert a tube called a catheter into the lungs. The catheter sends radiofrequency energy into the nerves outside the airways, then is removed from the body. If clinical trials find that the procedure helps people with their asthma without causing many complications or side effects, people will be able to get it done at a hospital. However, the medical trial process takes a long time, so it may be years before this happens.

A Useful Vitamin

Other scientists are investigating another treatment option that uses vitamin D. Vitamin D plays a crucial role in the development of the lungs and immune system, both of which could affect asthma symptoms. Multiple studies over many years have found evidence that increased levels of vitamin D can lessen asthma symptoms and severity.

Antibiotics and Asthma?

In 2017, a joint study published by numerous Australian universities reported that a common antibiotic was effective in reducing the severity of asthma attacks in their test groups. Azithromycin, the antibiotic that they studied, is used to treat a variety of issues, from ear infections to strep throat.

Between June 2009 and January 2015, more than 400 patients were randomly treated with either azithromycin or a placebo. By the end of their 48-week study, 95 percent of those in the antibiotic group reported a reduction in the severity of their asthma attacks. According to the researchers, the antibiotic alone may not control someone's asthma, but it "might be a useful add-on therapy in persistent asthma."[1]

1. P.G. Gibson et al., "Effect of Azithromycin on Asthma Exacerbations and Quality of Life in Adults with Persistent Uncontrolled Asthma (AMAZES): A Randomised, Double-Blind, Placebo-Controlled Trial," National Center for Biotechnology Information, *Lancet*, August 12, 2017. www.ncbi.nlm.nih.gov/pubmed/28687413.

One 2009 study, sponsored by the Children's Medical Center in Washington, D.C., measured the vitamin D blood levels of 85 African American children with asthma and 21 healthy African American children. The study found that the children with asthma were 20 times more likely to have low levels of vitamin D than the children without asthma. Another study, this one published in 2017, found that people who took vitamin D supplements along with their asthma medication "were 50 percent less likely to visit the emergency department or require hospital admission as a result of an asthma attack."[47] Additionally, the study found that the participants were less likely to need medication such as steroid injections after an asthma attack. So, although vitamin D is not a cure for asthma, people may benefit from adding a supplement or more foods rich in this particular vitamin to their diet.

It is possible that scientists may one day develop a cure for asthma, but in the meantime, if governments and world leaders can work together, the pollution that plagues the planet can be reduced—leading to a reduction in asthma cases. Although no treatment or medication currently available is 100 percent effective against asthma, the options that exist to help manage asthma can reduce the risk of a serious or deadly asthma attack. Through medications, new breathing techniques, reducing allergen exposure, and following asthma plans, the quality of life for people with asthma is better than ever before.

Fatty fish, cheese, and the yolks of eggs are all naturally rich in vitamin D, which may be linked to less severe asthma attacks.

Science, research, and observation are some of medicine's best tools right now. The studies that have been done—and that continue to be done—may lead scientists, researchers, and doctors to new innovations in treatments. Furthermore, the organizations that fight for cleaner air or improving access to asthma medications in schools have an important role to play as well. Anyone can advocate alongside these organizations to help people with asthma around the world.

NOTES

Introduction:
A Recurring Diagnosis

1. "Asthma Statistics," American Academy of Allergy Asthma & Immunology, accessed on March 7, 2018. www.aaaai.org/about-aaaai/ newsroom/asthma-statistics.

2. "Asthma Facts and Figures," Asthma and Allergy Foundation of America, last updated February 2018. www.aafa.org/page/asthma-facts. aspx.

3. "Asthma," World Health Organization, last updated April 2017. www.who.int/mediacentre/ factsheets/fs307/en.

Chapter One:
An Uncomfortable Attack

4. William E. Berger, *Asthma for Dummies*. Hoboken, NJ: Wiley Publishing, 2004, p. 12.

Chapter Two:
Identifying and Treating Asthma

5. S. Hasan Arshad and K. Suresh Babu, *The Facts: Asthma*. Oxford, UK: Oxford University Press, 2009, p. 51.

6. Berger, *Asthma for Dummies*, p. 35.

7. Genevieve Van Wyden, "Can Sage Brush Worsen Asthma Symptoms?," Health Guide Info, April 21, 2011. www.healthguideinfo. com/allergies-asthma-alternative-treatments/ p114782.

8. "Improving Access to Asthma Medications in Schools," American Lung Association, September 2014, p. 1. www.lung.org/assets/documents/asthma/improving-access-to-asthma.pdf.

9. "Improving Access," American Lung Association, p. 8.

10. "Improving Access," American Lung Association, p. 11.

11. Thomas F. Plaut, M.D., *One Minute Asthma*. Amherst, MA: Pedipress, Inc., 2008, p. 73.

12. Julia, interview by Barbara Sheen.

13. Quoted in "AANMA Clarifies FDA Asthma Medication Warnings," Occupational Health and Safety, February 26, 2010. ohsonline.com/Articles/2010/02/26/AANMA-Clarifies-FDA-Asthma-Medication-Warnings.aspx?admgarea=news&Page=2.

Chapter Three: Avoiding Asthma Triggers

14. Berger, *Asthma for Dummies*, p. 90.

15. Quoted in LeRoy M. Graham Jr. and Tim J. Vega, *The Essential Guide to the Management of Asthma*, ed. Stephen Brunton. Charlotte, NC: Primary Care Publications, 2011, p. 43. www.notonemorelife.org/userfiles/14/files/PCP%20Asthma%20Booklet%2010-26.pdf.

16. Berger, *Asthma for Dummies*, p. 92.

17. Elana Pearl Ben-Joseph, "Your House: How to Make It Asthma-Safe," KidsHealth, May 2017. kidshealth.org/en/kids/house-asthma.html.

18. Quoted in Melanie D. G. Kaplan, "Five Years Post-Katrina: Record Asthma Numbers Led to New Program," ZDNet, August 25, 2010.

www.zdnet.com/article/five-years-post-katrina-record-asthma-numbers-led-to-new-program.

19. Quoted in Lisa Belkin, "When Baby Is Allergic to Kitty," *New York Times*, March 19, 2010. parenting.blogs.nytimes.com/2010/03/19/when-baby-is-allergic-to-kitty.

20. Julia, interview.

21. Mattwire, "Living with Asthma: A Short Essay," Mattwire's Blog, July 2010. www.richmondjoke.typepad.com/blog/2010/07/living-with-asthma-a-short-essay.html.

22. Plaut, *One Minute Asthma*, p. 19.

23. Quoted in "St. Louis Ram Keenan Burton Tackling Asthma," Chris Draft Family Foundation, January 3, 2010. www.chrisdraftfamilyfoundation.org/news_media/articles?id=0117.

24. "Sports and Asthma: Mom I Can't Breathe," Everyday Health, August 16, 2007. www.everydayhealth.com/asthma/webcasts/sports-and-asthma-mom-i-cant-breathe.aspx.

25. Quoted in "Swimming Aids Asthma Symptoms in Children, Study Finds," Science Daily, August 27, 2009. www.sciencedaily.com/releases/2009/08/090824205522.htm.

Chapter Four:
Minimizing and Controlling Asthma Attacks

26. Plaut, *One Minute Asthma*, p. 28.

27. Wayne McCauley, "Asthma and Swimming: What Master Swimmers Need to Know," accessed on March 12, 2018. www.breaststroke.info/BRST12.htm.

28. Plaut, *One Minute Asthma*, p. 32.

29. Arshad and Babu, *The Facts: Asthma*, p. 103.

30. Quoted in Graham Jr. and Vega, *The Essential Guide to the Management of Asthma*, ed. Brunton, p. 43.

31. John Bottrell, "10 Things Not to Say to Someone Living with Asthma," Asthma.net, May 7, 2016. asthma.net/living/10-things-not-to-say-to-someone-living-with-asthma/comment-page-1/#comments.

32. Quoted in *Allergy and Asthma Today*, vol. 8, no. 2, p. 9. issuu.com/aanma/docs/aat_10_vol2.

33. Quoted in Sharon Kirkey, "Higher Asthma Rates Linked to Fast Food," Canada.com, January 27, 2009. www.canada.com/health/higher+asthma+rates+linked+fast+food/1223838/story.html.

34. Anne E. Dixon, "The Link Between Asthma and Weight," American Lung Association, last updated August 9, 2016. www.lung.org/about-us/blog/2016/07/the-link-between-asthma-weight.html.

35. Curt Cackovic and Rotimi Adigun, "Panic Disorder (Attack)," National Center for Biotechnology Information, last updated May 23, 2017. www.ncbi.nlm.nih.gov/books/NBK430973.

36. Carolyn Gregoire, "Here's How Meditation Reduces Inflammation and Prevents Disease," *Huffington Post*, February 8, 2016. www.huffingtonpost.com/entry/meditation-brain-changes-study_us_56b4b7aee4b04f9b57d93bef.

Chapter Five:
Asthma Today and Tomorrow

37. Quoted in Mandy Oaklander, "The Link Between Asthma and This Chemical," *TIME*,

October 7, 2014. time.com/3475859/bpa-lung-function-children.

38. "NCSL Policy Update: State Restrictions on Bisphenol A (BPA) in Consumer Products," National Conference of State Legislatures, February 2015. www.ncsl.org/research/environment-and-natural-resources/policy-update-on-state-restrictions-on-bisphenol-a.aspx.

39. "NCSL Policy Update," National Conference of State Legislatures.

40. Quoted in "Use of Acetaminophen in Pregnancy Associated with Increased Asthma Symptoms in Children," *(e)Science News*, February 4, 2010. www.esciencenews.com/articles/2010/02/04/use.acetaminophen.pregnancy.associated.with.increased.asthma.symptoms.children.

41. "New Study of the Potential Acetaminophen/Asthma Link," American Academy of Allergy Asthma & Immunology, October 28, 2014. www.aaaai.org/global/latest-research-summaries/Current-JACI-Research/acetaminophen-asthma.

42. Augusto A. Litonjua, "Acetaminophen and Asthma—A Small Sigh of Relief?," *New England Journal of Medicine*, August 18, 2016. www.nejm.org/doi/full/10.1056/NEJMe1607629.

43. Quoted in Steven Reinberg, "Prenatal Stress May Boost Baby's Asthma Risk," *HealthDay*, March 18 2010. consumer.healthday.com/respiratory-and-allergy-information-2/asthma-news-47/prenatalstress-may-boost-baby-s-asthma-risk-637111.html60.

44. Alison Lee et al., "Pre- and Postnatal Stress and Asthma in Children: Temporal- and Sex-Specific Associations," National Center for Biotechnology Information, *Journal of Allergy and Clinical Immunology*, vol. 138, no. 3, September 2016, pp. 740–747. www.ncbi.nlm.nih.gov/pmc/articles/PMC5011027.

45. Quoted in J. Faith Peppers, "Idling Buses Bad for Air, Kids," *Savannah Now*, July 28, 2010. www.savannahnow.com/article/20100728/NEWS/307289837.

46. Quoted in "Nuvaira Announces 1st Patient Treated in RELIEF-1 Study Evaluating New Approach for Asthma Treatment," *Globe NewsWire*, March 27, 2018. globenewswire.com/news-release/2018/03/27/1453546/0/en/Nuvaira-Announces-1st-Patient-Treated-in-RELIEF-1-Study-Evaluating-New-Approach-for-Asthma-Treatment.html.

47. Honor Whiteman, "Vitamin D Supplements May Reduce Asthma Severity," *Medical News Today*, October 4, 2017. www.medicalnewstoday.com/articles/319617.php.

allergen: A harmless substance, such as dust, that the body reacts to inappropriately.

alveoli: Air sacs in the lungs where oxygen and carbon dioxide are transferred in and out of the bloodstream.

antioxidant: A substance that helps the body's cells fight damage from oxygen molecules.

asthma action plan: A written plan that helps patients manage asthma symptoms.

asthmatic: Relating to asthma.

bronchial thermoplasty: An asthma treatment that uses radio waves to thin the muscle walls in airways.

bronchodilator: A commonly used medicine that opens the airways during an asthma attack.

corticosteroids: Drugs used to control inflammation.

inflammation: The body's defense against germs, characterized by heat, swelling, redness, and pain.

mucus: A thick, gooey substance produced by the respiratory system to trap irritants.

peak flow meter: A device people with asthma use to monitor their lung function.

spirometer: A device used by doctors to measure lung function.

wheeze: A whistling sound made when individuals try to force air through constricted airways.

American Academy of Allergy Asthma & Immunology
555 East Wells Street, Suite 1100
Milwaukee, WI 53202-3823
(414) 272-6071
www.aaaai.org
This organization provides a wide range of asthma
education and resources, as well as political advocacy
on health-related issues in Washington, D.C.

**American College of Allergies, Asthma
and Immunology**
85 West Algonquin Road, Suite 550
Arlington Heights, IL 60005
(847) 427-1200
www.acaai.org
The ACAAI provides allergy and asthma resources
to patients as well as practicing allergists. Its website
contains up-to-date research and developments, as well
as a symptom checker and a "find an allergist" tool.

The American Lung Association
American Lung Association's National Office
55 W. Wacker Drive, Suite 1150
Chicago, IL 60601
(800) 586-4872
info@lung.org
www.lungusa.org
The American Lung Association provides research and
community resources on everything from asthma to lung
cancer. It also supports new research and sponsors local
support groups.

Asthma and Allergy Foundation of America
8201 Corporate Drive, Suite 1000
Landover, MD 20785
(800) 727-8462
www.aafa.org
The AAFA provides information and social support
for allergy and asthma sufferers. People can also sign
up for its registry to become part of its data collection
for research.

National Jewish Health
1400 Jackson Street
Denver, CO 80206
(877) 225-5654
www.nationaljewish.org
This Denver hospital specializes in treating respiratory
illnesses and teamed up with the Icahn School of
Medicine at Mount Sinai in New York City to create
the Mount Sinai–National Jewish Health Respiratory
Institute. The hospital's website features a lot of
information and news about asthma.

Books

Cahill, Thomas A., Ph.D. *I Can Breathe Clearly Now: Protecting Yourself from Air Pollution*. Davis, CA: EditPros LLC, 2017.
This book gives readers tools and tips for reducing their exposure to air pollution daily.

Ford, Jean. *Allergies & Asthma*. Broomall, PA: Mason Crest Publishing, 2014.
This book helps readers learn about managing allergies and asthma to promote happier living.

Olle, David. *My Modern Health FAQs: Asthma*. Herndon, VA: Mercury Learning and Information, 2017.
The author presents answers to asthma-related questions in an engaging way with many available resources.

Yakoleva, Sasha, Konstantin Buteyko, and A. E. Novozhilov. *Breathe to Heal: Break Free from Asthma*. Lyons, CO: Breathing Center, LLC, 2016.
The authors describe different breathing techniques to reduce the discomfort of asthma attacks.

Zuchora-Walske, Christine. *Living with Asthma*. Minneapolis, MN: ABDO Publishing, 2014.
This book features stories about life with asthma along with explanations and advice from a medical expert.

Websites

BrainPop: Asthma

www.brainpop.com/health/diseasesinjuriesandconditions/ asthma

This section of the BrainPop website contains information, quizzes, activities, and games about asthma.

Breathe Easy, Play Hard

breatheeasyplayhard.com

This nonprofit organization is dedicated to supporting young athletes with asthma. It provides blogs about asthma, coping skills for athletes with asthma, and information and interviews with professional athletes with asthma.

CDC: Asthma

www.cdc.gov/asthma

This website offers links to statistics and data trend reports, as well as links to other national agencies involved in asthma research and advocacy.

TeensHealth: Asthma

teenshealth.org/en/teens/asthma.html

TeensHealth provides information about health concerns, including asthma, for teachers, parents, and teenagers.

World Health Organization: Asthma

www.who.int/respiratory/asthma/en

The WHO webpage on chronic respiratory diseases includes fact sheets as well as tips for living a healthy, happy life with asthma.

INDEX

ABOUT THE AUTHOR

Peter Kogler is a schoolteacher in Buffalo, New York. When he is not teaching, he loves to write, collect old toys, and read everything he can get his hands on. Staying up to date on current events and research in the medical and science fields is incredibly fascinating to him. This is his first educational book, and he hopes that people enjoy reading it as much as he did writing it.